The Qur'an Discussions

Also by Ahmed Lotfy Rashed

What Would a Muslim Say?
Top 15 Tough Questions on Islam

The Qur'an Discussions
What Would a Muslim Say
Volume 2

by

Ahmed Lotfy Rashed

Common Word Publishing
"With Dialogue Comes Understanding"

Copyright

Copyright © 2017 by Ahmed Lotfy Rashed

All rights reserved. This book or any portion thereof may not be reproduced or used in any manner whatsoever without the express written permission of the publisher, except for the use of brief quotations in a book review.

Editing: Allister Thompson

Cover Design: Stewart Williams

ISBN–13: 978-0999431801

Dedication

In the Name of God,
the Most-Gracious,
the Ever-Merciful.

Acknowledgments

There are many people to thank for this book.

First, I thank my mother for teaching me to always be patient, even if it is uncomfortable. And I thank my father for teaching me to always be truthful, even if it is unpopular.

Second, I thank my wife for her patience, support, and encouragement as I navigated each conversation.

Last, but certainly not least, I want to thank the shining models from whom I consulted or referenced for the more nuanced or detailed answers that I had to provide: Yasir Qadhi, Gai Eaton, Zaid Shakir, Hamza Yusuf, Nouman Ali Khan, Suhaib Webb, Sherman Jackson, and Jamal Badawi. May God bless you all and preserve your teachings for all students of Islam.

Contents

Copyright iv
Dedication v
Acknowledgments vi
Contents vii
Introduction 3
God's Grace and Free Will 5
Islamic Financing and Celibacy 17
Plural Wives, Orphans, and Slavery 23
Inheritance and Adultery 29
Scripture and Divine Decree 43
On Hypocrites 49
Plural Wives Revisited and Islamic Criminal Law 55
Interfaith Friendships and the Status of Jews in Islam 59
On Sacrifices and Sleeping Souls 71
Prophet Ibrahim and the Future of Islam 75
The Jinn, the Devil, and Paradise 79
Faith, Reason, and the Nature of Adam 85
The People of *A'raf* and the Previous Arabs 93
The Sabbath and Islamic Asceticism 99
The Verse of the Sword 111
The Holy Months and Charity 119
Pharaoh, Jonah, Jacob, and Joseph 125
The Canonical Texts of Islam 131
A Message From the Author 139
Interfaith Dialogues and Debates 141
About the Author xii

TOUGH QUESTIONS AND HONEST ANSWERS ABOUT THE WORLD'S FASTEST-GROWING AND MOST CONTROVERSIAL FAITH.

TOP 15 TOUGH QUESTIONS ON ISLAM

AHMED LOTFY RASHED

Get your FREE copy when you sign up to the author's email list!

GET IT HERE:
WhatWouldAMuslimSay.net

MY TEACHER WAS AHMED RASHED. WE SPENT A LOT OF TIME GOING THROUGH THE QUR'AN. AFTER THAT I STARTED TO UNDERSTAND MUSLIMS MUCH BETTER.
—FORMER ISLAM-101 STUDENT

The Qur'an Discussions

Introduction

Introduction

The Conversation with Winston

This book contains conversations with one of the people who reached out to WhyIslam.org for dialogue and received me as their correspondent. WhyIslam conversations typically begin when a person visits the WhyIslam website and submits a "One to One Email Correspondence" form. From this form, the Correspondence Manager assigns the visitor to one of the WhyIslam volunteers. If the visitor is assigned to me, the questions or comments are delivered to my email, and then I initiate the first email to reach out and respond to the visitor's questions. The conversation then flows from there, just like a print letter correspondence.

We met Winston in my first book, **What Would Muslim Say?** Winston asked many questions of a deep nature over the course of nine months as he read through the Qur'an. This conversation was one of the most complex, intricate, and extensive exchanges I have ever had in my volunteer work. For this reason, the entire book consists of that single back-and-forth conversation with Winston.

However, unlike the first book, the chapter breaks of this book represent different discussion topics as Winston and I read through the Qur'an. Note that Winston broke off the conversation soon after completing Chapter 13. This is actually very common; as I mentioned in my last email to him, the first third of the Qur'an is where most of the social, legal, and political rulings reside, so it is this section of the Qur'an that generates most questions and discussions. The remaining two thirds deal more with the stories of the previous Prophets and spiritual and moral admonitions.

God's Grace and Free Will

God's Grace and Free Will

Email #02 – From: Winston
Sent: Wednesday, February 22, 2011 5:15 p.m.

I have two questions about verses in the Qur'an: 1) V2:6 and V2:7 (i.e., in the second Surah on verse six and seven) appears to mean that the reason people disbelieve in Islam is because Allah desires it, but if that is true then people do not have any free will to accept or reject Islam. Do human beings have complete free will, or is it limited, or is there none? 2) Regarding V2:24, does this statement mean that anyone who is not a Muslim will be punished by Allah? If this is true, then are non-Muslims who have good thoughts and perform good deeds, also going to be punished after death? In other words, is it possible to be a good person and not be a Muslim?

Email #03 – From: Ahmed Rashed
Sent: Wednesday, February 23, 2011 6:26 a.m.

In the Name of God, the Most-Gracious, the Ever-Merciful:
Hello Winston,

Your first question regarding (2:6-7) refers to the leaders of Quraysh who had heard the Prophet's preaching for over thirteen years and still refused to accept that he was truly sent by God. In addition to refusing belief, they used their power and influence to prevent others from believing in the Prophet. This prevention took the form of persecution, verbal, and physical abuse, economic boycott, and beatings, torture, and killing. These opening verses were revealed in the first few years after the Prophet migrated from Mecca to Medina (twelve to thirteen years after first receiving revelation), and their purpose was to console the Prophet, for he was eager for all the people to believe and follow the guidance he was sent with. God informed him that none would believe except those who received God's grace.

The Qur'an teaches that God guides those who *want* to be guided and leaves astray those who *do not wish to receive guidance*, like the leaders of Quraysh referred to in (2:6-7).

We read this in the Qur'an: **Then when they turned away, God turned their hearts away. (61:5)**

But because they broke their covenant, We cursed them, and made their hearts grow hard. (5:13)

God's granting or withholding His grace is a result of the heart **choosing** to turn toward Him or away from Him. If the choices we made were *not* genuine, it would be **injustice** for God to hold us accountable for them. Since God is *The Just, The Forbearing,* and *The Truth,* we understand that our choices are real. The Qur'an affirms this by ending in many different verses with the following phrase: **This is for what you yourself have done, and never is God unjust to His creatures.**

As for your second question, the verse (2:23-24) is simply a challenge to those who doubt that the Qur'an is really from God. It says to compose a chapter as eloquent and profound. Since the Arabs were at the peak of their literary abilities at that time, and since Muhammad was a simple, illiterate man never known for any poetic ability in the forty years of life before revelation, the challenge is a strong one even in this day and age.

As for your question about what happens to non-Muslims, the Qur'an says: **And whoever seeks a religion other than Islam, it will not be accepted from him, and he will be one of the losers in the Hereafter. (3:85)**

This may seem extreme, but as mentioned in the first email, it is written in the Qur'an that God sent Prophets to each nation in history. In other words, God made a covenant with every people in every time. This covenant was "Islam," which means surrender and obedience to God, and a person who surrenders his will to God and obeys His commandments is called a "Muslim." The primary condition for salvation is faith in God and directing all worship exclusively to God.

This understanding is confirmed by the Qur'an: **The believers, the Jews, the Christians, and the Sabians — all who believed in God and the Last Day and do good deeds — will be rewarded by their Lord; they shall have no fear, nor shall they grieve. (2:62)**

This means that those from the previous nations, who faithfully followed the AUTHENTIC teachings of their Prophets (Jesus, Moses, Abraham, etc.), will receive God's mercy and forgiveness.

As for those who never met a Prophet, let me show you a quote from Dr. Sherman Jackson, a well-known Muslim scholar at the University of California. He translated many classical books and is well respected in the field. In his introduction to Imam Al-Ghazali's famous book, *Theological Tolerance*, Dr. Jackson explains this issue as follows:

Al-Ghazali goes on, however, to insist that God's mercy will encompass non-Muslims as well, including "most of the Christians of Byzantium and the [non-Muslim] Turks of the age." These people he divides into three categories: 1) those who never heard so much as the name Muhammad; 2) those who heard his name and had access to concrete and authentic information about his life and mission; 3) those who heard of him but received wrong, insufficient, or misleading information about this life and mission. According to al-Ghazali, it is only those of the second category, those who came into reliable and concrete information about Muhammad and, in a spirit of defiance, persist in rejecting his Prophethood, which will dwell forever in Hellfire. This is because only such people can be said to be guilty of deeming the Prophet to be a liar. As for those of the first and third categories, these will be covered by God's all-encompassing mercy. For, ultimately, their non-acceptance of Muhammad's Prophethood is free of defiance and attributable to circumstances beyond their control.

Let me know if you would like more in-depth information or if you have any follow-up questions. I look forward to your response, Winston, and I hope to continue the discussion.

May peace be with you,
Ahmed Rashed

Email #04 – From: Winston
Sent: Friday, February 25, 2011 11:43 a.m.

Hello,

Thank you for taking time from your busy schedule to respond to my email. Could you please help me understand these two verses from the Qur'an? (1) Regarding V2:34, do angels have free will? If angels do not have free will, then how can Iblis choose to reject Allah? If angels are free to reject or accept Islam, then what happens to all the angels who rejected it? (2) Regarding V2:61, who were the Sabians? Do the Sabians still exist now?

Always Grateful,
Winston

Email #05 – From: Ahmed Rashed
Sent: Friday, February 25, 2011 3:42 p.m.

In the Name of God, the Most-Gracious, the Ever-Merciful:

No problem, Winston; I am glad to be of service. To proceed with your questions:

The angels are intelligent beings that God created from light. They are luminous creatures with no physical bodies. They do not eat, drink, or procreate; they are above animal desires, sins, and mistakes. They do not have human characteristics, but they can, with God's permission, appear in the form of human beings. They are not gods, nor are they the sons or daughters of God. The relationship of the angels to God is that of absolute service, obedience, and submission to His commands. They do not have free will and are in constant submission to God, carrying out His work and executing His commands as He pleases.

So If Angels cannot disobey God, what about Satan?

Satan — whose name in Arabic is "Iblis"—questioned God's appointment of fallible humans to the honorable position of stewardship. Iblis disobeyed God and refused to prostrate himself to Adam. The Qur'an says: **When We said to the angels, 'Prostrate yourselves before Adam,' all prostrated themselves**

God's Grace and Free Will

except Satan. He was one of the jinn and he disobeyed his Lord's command. Do you then take him and his offspring as protectors instead of Me, despite their enmity? What an evil exchange for the wrongdoers! (18:50)

This is one difference between the Biblical and Qur'anic narrative. Iblis is not an angel or a fallen angel. Angels cannot disobey God, so angels cannot fall. Satan was from the Jinn, described in the Qur'an in this passage: **We created man out of dry clay, from molded mud, and the Jinn We had created before from flaming fire. (15:26-27)**

So the Jinn are a creation that is part of the Unseen World, like angels, but they are able to choose between obedience and disobedience like men. There are good, believing Jinn and evil, wicked Jinn. To understand the relationship between Jinn and Men, we continue reading this passage from the Qur'an: **Your Lord said to the angels, "I am about to bring into being a man wrought from mud. When I have formed him and breathed My spirit into him, fall down in prostration before him," then the angels all prostrated themselves together. But Satan did not; he refused to join those who prostrated themselves.**

God asked him, "What is the matter with you that you are not among those who have prostrated themselves?" He replied, "I am not one to prostrate myself to a man whom You have created out of clay of molded mud."

God said, "Then get out of here; for you are accursed, and the curse shall be on you till the Day of Judgment!" Satan said, "O my Lord! Grant me respite till the Day of Resurrection." He said, "You are granted respite till that Appointed Day." He said, "My Lord, since You have let me go astray, I shall beautify for them the path of evil on earth and I shall mislead them all, except for Your chosen servants."

God said, "This is the path which leads straight to Me. Surely, you shall have no power over My true servants, except the misguided who choose to follow you. Surely, Hell is the place to which they are destined." (15:28-43)

So the first source of evil is Satan, and all the evil, wicked Jinn that follow him; they spend their days and nights whispering suggestions into the hearts of Adam's progeny. The other source of evil is the selfish inclination of the soul of the person itself. The satanic forces are defeated by constant remembrance, repentance, and prayer. The selfish forces are defeated by worship, discipline, obeying God's commands, and living the Prophetic lifestyle.

As for the Sabians in the other verse, there are two interpretations that the classical commentators mention. The first one (slight in the majority) is that they are a subgroup of People of the Book — not Jews, not Christians, and not around anymore. The second one (a slight minority) is that they are any people who reject the established organized religions of their society and turn to direct worship of God without any Prophet or Scripture to follow. This second opinion includes people who lived after the time of Prophet Muhammad but never heard of his message or the Qur'an or met any Muslims.

May peace be with you,
Ahmed

Email #06 – From: Winston
Sent: Friday, March 4, 2011 8:03 a.m.

Hello Ahmed,

Thank you for responding to my previous questions. Could you please help me to understand the following verses from the Qur'an? (1) Regarding V2:74, what is the meaning of this metaphor? (2) Regarding V2:88, what exactly is the curse Allah has placed on the Jewish people? If Allah has placed a curse on all Jewish people, then that means the unborn children of future generations will get the curse. However, according to V2:286 (if I read it correctly) each person is responsible for their own sins.

How can one group of people be cured throughout time for the sins made by those in the distant past? V2:286 is the following:

God's Grace and Free Will

God does not burden a soul beyond capacity. Each will enjoy what (good) he earns, as indeed each will suffer from (the wrong) he does. Punish us not, O Lord, if we fail to remember or lapse into error. Burden us not, O Lord, with a burden as You did those before us. Impose not upon us a burden, O Lord, we cannot carry. Overlook our trespasses and forgive us, and have mercy upon us; You are our Lord and Master, help us against the clan of unbelievers.

The translation is from *Al-Qur'an* by Ahmed Ali.
Always Grateful,
Winston

Email #07 – From: Ahmed Rashed
Sent: Tuesday, March 8, 2011 10:42 a.m.

In the Name of God, the Most-Gracious, the Ever-Merciful:

Hello Winston,

So regarding 2:74, this verse is saying that the hearts of these people became not just "as hard as a rock" but rather became "harder than rock." For it is an observable fact that some rocks are split by rivers that run through them (canyons and waterfalls come to mind), and other rocks are split by even smaller amounts of water (think of mudslides or streams that happen just after a rain), and other rocks crack/split on their own. So each metaphor shows a rock splitting due to weaker and weaker impact (river, rain, on-their-own), and therefore the comparison is that the hearts of these men who witnessed a miracle of resurrection and still were obstinate are even harder than rocks.

As for 2:88, this is referring to the immediate community of those who denied and/or killed prophets before and were threatening to do the same to Prophet Muhammad. Every human being, regardless of his upbringing or parents' religion, has a chance to learn the truth and accept it. However, the curse does not fall except on those who received signs and prophets and still refuse to accept. Notice that v2:87 talks about those who denied Moses and Jesus, whereas v2:88-89 talk about those who denied

Muhammad. This means those who WITNESSED and MET these great prophets and still chose to not follow them for some contrived reason. This is indicated by the verse: **Is it ever so, that, when there cometh unto you a Messenger with that which ye yourselves desire not, ye grow arrogant and some ye disbelieve and some ye slay? (2:87)**

May peace be with you,
Ahmed

Email #08 – From: Winston
Sent: Wednesday, March 9, 2011 9:08 a.m.

Hello Ahmed,

Thank you for responding to my previous questions. However, you did not completely answer my second question. Verse 2:88 in the Qur'an mentions a curse. The verse seems to imply that the curse is that *a person will not believe in Islam completely or at all*. But this is really the cause, not the effect of the curse. Otherwise, if the **act of disbelieving** is itself a curse of Allah, then it is not the people who are choosing to accept or reject Islam. Since people have free will, that is they can make decisions without Allah interfering, then the curse must be something else. Can you define, in detail, what the curse is?

Always Grateful,
Winston

Email #09 – From: Ahmed Rashed
Sent: Monday, March 14, 2011 12:27 p.m.

In the Name of God, the Most-Gracious, the Ever-Merciful:

Hello Winston,

First of all, I apologize for the delay in responding. Let us start with an excerpt from our Islam101 lecture about Divine Decree, Destiny, and Grace:

Islam teaches that God, The Giver, has honored humanity with the ability to choose between right and wrong. This gift comes with great responsibility, and we will be accountable for our use of this gift on Judgment Day.

Human free will does not contradict the fact that God, The Witness, knows everything that will ever occur in creation. Some might say, "If God knows I am going to commit a sin tomorrow, then it is unavoidable because what God knows will come to pass." Islam teaches that God's knowledge of our decision is a consequence of his being The All-Knowing, not a consequence of our being forced to make that decision. His knowledge is perfect and infinite; therefore it is illogical that anything could be hidden from Him or surprising to Him.

Human free will does not contradict the fact that nothing happens in creation except what God wills. Some might say, "Therefore, I have no free will; it is just an illusion." Islam teaches that God created within each of us the **ability** to formulate an intention. God wants us to be able to make our own choices. When a person makes a choice, God, by His divine will, creates the actions and circumstances that allow or disallow the person's intention to be carried out.

What this all means is that God guides those who want to be guided and leaves astray those who do not wish to receive guidance. We read this in the Qur'an: **Then when they turned away, God turned their hearts away (61:5)**

But because they broke their covenant, We cursed them, and made their hearts grow hard. (5:13)

Now let us dig into the translation a little bit. The actual words used in the verse mentioned is **"la-a-na,"** which is usually translated as "he cursed." The opposite word linguistically is **"na-a-ma,"** which is usually translated as "he graced." What I am trying to point out is that just as God bestows his Grace on those who seek Him and turn to Him, He also withholds His Grace from those who deny Him or consistently turn away from Him. That is the Islamic understanding of God's "curse."

So those who continue to turn away and disobey and defy God time and time again will eventually seal themselves off from God's Grace. This is supported by many sayings of the Prophet, many verses in the Qur'an, and many sayings of the scholars as well. God's Grace and mercy is open to any and all who come to

Him with sincerity and humility. But those who do not come to him, or do so with arrogance or some sense of entitlement, will not receive God's Grace.

More importantly for our discussion, when a human being exercises his free will time and time again to turn away from God's Grace, then **and only then** does God decree this person to be beyond redemption. In other words, God has sealed his fate. However, this decree of God is not arbitrary, nor is it tyrannical, for it is the many actions of the free agent human being himself that has sealed his own fate. It is the accumulation of unrepented sins that result in that person being cut off from God's Grace.

This concept is similar to the Old Testament description of Pharaoh in the story of Moses. It is said of Pharaoh that "his heart was hardened." Again, who hardened his heart? Obviously, God (who has power over all things) is the one who hardened his heart. But what is the cause of this hardening? It is nothing more than the defiance and arrogance of Pharaoh himself.

God never withholds His Grace the first time a person sins or defies Him, nor the second, nor the 10th, nor even the 100th. It is when sinning and defiance and arrogance become that person's way of life of that God makes his Decree.

It is this kind of people that the verse is referencing. Feel free to contact me with more questions along this line, or if you have other topics you would like to discuss.

May peace be with you,
Ahmed

With Dialogue Comes Understanding

ISLAMIC FINANCING AND CELIBACY

Islamic Financing and Celibacy

Email #10 – From: Winston
Sent: Tuesday, March 15, 2011 9:22 p.m.

Hello Ahmed,

Thank you. Your response to my last question was very enlightening. You do not need to apologize for any delay. I appreciate any effort you can make to answer my questions. Can you please help me to understand the following verses?

(1) Regarding verse 2:275, is the act of earning interest forbidden by Allah? If this is true, then having a savings account with a bank, owning stocks on Wall Street, a career in the financial industry, etc., is also forbidden.

(2) Regarding verse 3:39, this verse seems to state that the Prophet 'Isa (peace be upon him) will practice celibacy. Is there any passage in the Qur'an which mentions that 'Isa (peace be upon him) was married? There are none in the third sura. From what I understand of Islam, each Prophet of Allah (peace be upon them) is a role model of a Muslim, and all Muslims must emulate them as much as possible. If it is true that 'Isa (peace be upon him) had intentionally chosen not to get married, then all Muslims must practice celibacy.

Always Grateful,
Winston

Email #11 – From: Ahmed Rashed
Sent: Friday, March 18, 2011 11:31 a.m.

In the Name of God, the Most-Gracious, the Ever-Merciful:

Hello Winston,

It seems you are reading through the Qur'an and asking questions along the way. Is this so, or are you doing a focused study? To proceed with your questions:

(1) Interest is forbidden, whether giving or taking. So yes, all the things you list are also forbidden. The Prophet also predicted that there would come a day when nobody would be safe from his/her wealth being tainted by interest in some way or

form. Most scholars believe this prediction to be actualized in this day of interest-based financing and debt-based economy.

One small clarification: there is nothing intrinsically forbidden about owning stock in a company and trading these stocks/shares on the open market. What makes it forbidden is the fact that every business in the market puts its money in interest-bearing accounts for savings, investments, and so on. So any return on investment, profit-sharing, or capital gains are tainted with interest, which gets passed on the shareholder.

(2) No. First of all, this verse refers to the son of Zachariah, not Jesus. In the Qur'an, the son of Zachariah is called Yahya; in the Bible, he is called John the Baptist.

The Prophet predicted that when Jesus returns to earth, he will come as a ruler. He will establish justice, marry, have children, and then die a natural death. There is no contradiction between Yahya being unmarried and Muslims being encouraged to marry. Why? For one thing, Yahya never commanded people to abstain from marriage. For another thing, the final messenger's teachings supersede any previous prophet's teachings.

It has always been the case that a prophet would inform his followers which of his practices are mandatory to emulate and which are praiseworthy but only binding on himself. For example, the Prophet Muhammad always prayed long hours before dawn. This prayer is praiseworthy for Muslims, but it was not mandatory. Also, the wives of the Prophet were required to cover their faces (the **niqab** or face-veil). This is a virtuous act for other Muslim women, but it is not mandatory.

May peace be with you,
Ahmed

Email #12 – From: Winston
Sent: Monday, March 21, 2011 8:10 a.m.

Hello Ahmed,

Thank you for responding to my previous questions. My intention was to read the entire Qur'an, but that is not possible at this time because I do not know how to read classical Arabic. As you already know, when the Qur'an is translated into another language then it is no longer the Qur'an. The best I can do now is to read a decent translation and verify, with a Muslim who can read the Qur'an in classical Arabic, the basic meaning of the verses. Before I began this correspondence, I had assumed that the organization WhyIslam.com had volunteers who can actually read the Qur'an. If the organization did not, then it would be like the blind leading the blind. Can you please help me to understand the following verses in the Qur'an?

(1) Regarding verse 2:275, you had mentioned in the previous email that interest is forbidden and the stock market is tainted with interest. If a soup contained one percent of pork, then the entire soup is forbidden because the possibly of eating pork, which Allah has forbidden, would be so high that it is almost unavoidable. Based on this logic, a pious Muslim will have to do business only with a bank that does not charge interest or earn a profit from it. Furthermore, he or she would have to refrain from investing in the stocks and other financial products. Are there any halal financial institutions in North America? If there are none in North America, then a pious Muslim would have to hide all his money in his home.

(2) Regarding verses 3:37, 3:38, 3:39, and 3:40, was Maryam married to Zachariah, or did Zachariah become Maryam's stepfather who raised her? If the Prophets Yahya and 'Isa (peace be upon them) are in the family of Imran, then how are they related to each other?

May peace be with you,
Winston

Email #13 – From: Ahmed Rashed
Sent: Wednesday, March 23, 2011 5:10 p.m.

In the Name of God, the Most-Gracious, the Ever-Merciful:
Hello Winston,

Good to see you are making your way slowly through the Qur'an. To proceed with your questions:

1. Islamic transaction law is complicated, so I will try to break it down for you. Investing and profit-sharing is permissible and encouraged. Many Muslims do this sort of thing with each other if they know that the business owner X is an observant Muslim who does not pay or receive interest in the course of running their business. So observant Muslims would invest money with X, and when X does his accounts at the end of the term, he divides his profits into the shares of those who gave him capital (just like stock shares and dividend returns).

Now let's say business owner Y is not an observant Muslim (or not a Muslim at all), and he pays or gets interest all over the place. It is NOT permissible to invest or profit-share with Y, because any return would be tainted with interest. However, it is perfectly OK to buy whatever product or service Y sells as long as that product or service is permissible.

This is the example of modern interest-based banks. Observant Muslims would obviously prefer a bank based on Islamic principles, but these are few and far between. Therefore, they will use a conventional bank only for their checking accounts. The checking account must be non-interest-bearing, of course, but that is the only requirement for the observant Muslim to open an account with a clear conscience. The fact that the bank makes its money off of loans is irrelevant. The sin is on the bank, not on the checking account holder.

For example, a 7-Eleven store sells many products, some of which are not permissible for an observant Muslim to buy (like tobacco, alcohol, or lottery tickets), and some of the products are permissible for an observant Muslim to buy (like candy, soda, and milk). Just because a company sells some forbidden products, it does not mean I cannot buy permissible products from them. Furthermore, imagine a company that sells nothing but permissible products, but its finances are filled with interest. I can buy whatever I want from them, but I cannot invest in that company.

So as I said before, it is not the stock market that is tainted with interest... it is the businesses that are in the stock market that are tainted. By the way, there is in fact a Dow Jones Islamic Index in which some Muslims invest. This index is not completely interest-free, though. Since Islamic financing is still such a young discipline, scholars have allowed some leeway to allow the Muslim businesses to catch up with the world markets. Scholars use the analogy of "tainted water" from classical Islamic jurisprudence to allow these stocks to be traded in. Just as water is still considered pure (you can drink it) if the impurity in the water is below a certain amount, so too a business is considered pure (you can invest in it) if the interest in their finances is below a certain amount.

The idea is that having an Islamic Index would reward businesses for "low-interest" operation and thereby encourage business owners (Muslim and non-Muslim) to drive their businesses to "no-interest" operation.

However, most conservative Muslims do not invest in these securities and funds because they do not feel comfortable with this "tolerated" approach and would rather not have any interest mixed in their wealth. For this reason, most conservative Muslims invest their money either by purchasing gold and silver or investing with small Muslim businesses that they personally know are interest-free.

2. As for Isa's family relationship: Maryam's mother and Zachariah's wife were sisters. So that makes Zachariah the uncle of Maryam (by marriage not by blood). So Yahya is Maryam's first cousin. Yahya is Isa's first cousin, once removed.

May peace be with you,
Ahmed

Plural Wives, Orphans, and Slavery

Plural Wives, Orphans, and Slavery

Email #14 – From: Winston
Sent: Friday, March 25, 2011 11:49 a.m.

Hello Ahmed,

Thank you for responding to my previous questions. Can you please help me to understand the following verse in the Qur'an?

(1) Regarding verse 4:3, is a Muslim man limited to marrying only four women? If the Muslim man is allowed to marry more than four, then is there any limit to the number of wives he can have?

(2) According to verse 4:3, a Muslim man is required to treat his wives equally. Are there rules in the Qur'an, Hadith (or Sunnah), Sharia (I know this is not a source of Islam but are laws derived from the Qur'an and Hadith) that details how exactly a Muslim man is supposed to treat his multiple wives equally? Do not list every single law regarding this issue. I am only asking if these laws exist, because if equity in marriage is not defined, then an immoral husband could justify oppressing or abusing his wives with the excuse of ambiguous rules.

Note: I am aware that Shia and Sunni Islam have their own Hadith collections and thus each will have their own version of Sharia. In order to avoid the unnecessary complexly of answering questions in two different ways, please interpret all my questions in a Sunni Islamic way.

May peace be with you,
Winston

Email #15 – From: Ahmed Rashed
Sent: Monday, March 28, 2011 5:54 p.m.

In the Name of God, the Most-Gracious, the Ever-Merciful:
Hello Winston,

1. Yes, four is the maximum number of wives a Muslim man can marry at any given time.

2. Yes, there are rules for equal treatment. These include

equal time, separate but equal living quarters, and equal accompaniment when traveling. These rules were directly observed from the life of the Prophet with his wives. He would spend each night with a different wife; he would house each wife in her own private apartment that was the same size as all other apartments; and when travelling he would draw lots to decide which wife would travel with him. Islamic scholars later codified these into more specific guidelines and rights.

May peace be with you,
Ahmed

Email #16 – From: Winston
Sent: Wednesday, March 30, 2011 5:56 p.m.

Hello Ahmed,

Thank you for responding to my previous questions. Could you please help to understand the following verses from the Qur'an.

(1) Regarding verses 4:3 and 4:24, it is mentioned that a Muslim man can marry women who are captured. Are these verses referring to incidents when the first generation of Muslims when to war with the pagan Arabs and captured their women after winning a battle? If women were captured, then forced to marry Muslim men, this would be slavery. Do these two verses permit Muslims to own slaves? If not, then does Allah permit slavery anywhere in the Qur'an?

(2) Regarding verse 4:6, what age does an orphan female have to be in order to get married? If children are allowed to marry, then that is immoral because children are too immature to make important decisions, and thus they are being taken advantage of. Furthermore, if adults are being allowed to marry children, that is even worse.

May peace be with you,
Winston

Email #17 – From: Ahmed Rashed
Sent: Sunday, April 3, 2011 8:18 a.m.

In the Name of God, the Most-Gracious, the Ever-Merciful:
Hello Winston,
Regarding your first question:
Slavery already existed long before Islam. It was a system whereby a human captured in wars or kidnapped could be sold as a "possession." That term applied to both sexes, not to women only. In some cultures slaves were considered subhuman and treated brutally. In Europe, for example, Romans threw Christian slaves to the lions while the public cheered; female slaves were thought to have no souls and were tortured mercilessly; slaves lived in degrading conditions; both sexes were forced to offer sexual favors to their masters; and as "possessions" they had no choice, no will, and no rights.

While it did not abolish slavery completely, Islam did restrict the way slaves could be acquired to only one way: captives of war. In addition, it recognized the human rights of slaves and mandated humane treatment for them:

Narrated Al-Ma'rur: *At Ar-Rabadha, I met Abu Dhar who was wearing a cloak, and his slave, too, was wearing a similar one. I asked about the reason for it. He replied, "I abused a person by calling his mother with bad names." The Prophet said to me, 'O Abu Dhar! Did you abuse him by calling his mother with bad names? You still have some characteristics of ignorance.* **Your slaves are your brothers** *and Allah has put them under your command. So whoever has a brother under his command should feed him of what he eats and dress him of what he wears. Do not ask them (slaves) to do things beyond their capacity (power), and if you do so, then help them.*

In addition, Islam put in place incentives for the eventual removal of the institution of slavery. It did this by encouraging Muslims to set slaves free, as you read in 2:177, and as is mentioned in many chapters as expiation for various sins. In this way, it declared the moral status of treating slaves well and declared the virtue and heavenly reward for freeing them. The

Prophet forbade his Companions from harming or abusing their slaves, and the Qur'an explicitly prohibits forcing female slaves into sexual acts against their will (see 24:32-34). Instead of concubines and sex-slaves, the Prophet encouraged educating them, setting them free, then legally marrying them and giving them their moral and financial rights.

Regarding your second question:

Chapter 4, verse 6 is not about female orphans. It is about orphans in general. The explicit meaning of the text is that orphans should be given their money when they reach the "marriageable age"; however, the implied or commonly-understood meaning of the text is that orphans should be given their money when they are actually about to get married. The wisdom behind this is to prevent prodigal children from getting wealth all at once. A person who gets suddenly rich usually is not responsible with the new wealth. So Islam teaches that the wealth should be given when they have proven themselves capable of holding responsibility (marriage). As for the marriage age, Islam requires that both the bride and groom to be 1) past puberty, 2) capable of handling the responsibilities of marriage, as judged by their parents or guardians, and 3) consenting to the union.

Young marriages were common because people matured quickly. Life was hard, so there was not much time for extended childhood and lack of responsibilities like in the modern age. I know that in my grandparents' generation, for example, boys and girls were expected to work and help the family around the farm or the shop when they were seven or eight. My wife's grandmother got married when she was twelve. This was no injustice, because she'd already been "a full woman" for two years, and she was emotionally and mentally prepared for marriage because life in the farm was demanding and all children had to assume responsibility at an early age to survive. So the point is that as long as person is physically and emotionally and mentally capable of the rights and responsibilities of marriage, it is permissible for them to get married. Even today, my wife's nephews routinely are sent to go around the block buy whatever their mother needs for that day. They are only three years old, but they can navigate crossing streets and asking directions and paying for the goods and getting the correct change. It is all a matter of upbringing and how soon you entrust a child with responsibility.

    May peace be with you,
    Ahmed

Inheritance and Adultery

Inheritance and Adultery

Email #18 – From: Winston
Sent: Monday, April 4, 2011 11:10 a.m.

Hello Ahmed,

Thank you for responding to my previous questions. Could you please help me to understand the following verses from the Qur'an:

(1) Regarding verse 4:11, it mentions that Muslim men must receive a significantly larger inheritance than women. For that reason, the Islamic system of inheritance appears to be oppressive to women because it gives people an advantage based on how they born. No one can control how they are born. Throughout history, with a few exceptions, women were completely dependent on men to survive because of the economic and political circumstances of their society. However, in the past hundred years many nations have reformed their laws to enable men and women to have an equal amount of economic and political power. Although women are physically weaker than men and thus would need to depend on men, most modern occupations do not require physical strength. Education and technical skill is what will determine survival in the modern world. I recognize the fact that in early human history people had to rely on their physical ability far more than their intellectual ability, but technological advances have reduce the importance of physical capability. This has resulted in women being able to compete with men economically and politically, if they are given the opportunity. If Islam is a religion for all mankind in every time period, how can the Islamic system of inheritance be fair when compared to the gender equality of modern times?

(2) Regarding verses 4:15 and 4:16, do these two passages state that homosexual and lesbian behavior is forbidden? If this is not true, then what is the meaning of these verses?

May peace be with you,
Winston

Email #19 – From: Ahmed Rashed
Sent: Monday, April 4, 2011 3:53 p.m.

In the Name of God, the Most-Gracious, the Ever-Merciful:
Hello Winston,

(1) When considering this law, one must keep in mind the whole Islamic economic system, of which inheritance law is just one aspect. Men bear the sole burden of financially supporting every member of the family. In essence, the money a man earns or inherits is not his alone, but belongs to the whole family. Women have the freedom and right to work and receive earnings. However, they are not legally obligated to spend any of their money on the family's needs, even if they are doctors in a high-tech society.

The same is true of inheritance. The men of the family are obligated to use any income, including inheritance, to provide financial support to the entire family. Women receive their inheritance with no strings attached, no financial obligations to fulfill. Therefore, Muslims see it as only fair that the amounts be adjusted to reflect this reality.

In addition, this ruling is applied only in one specific instance: when children (brothers and sisters) are inheriting from their parents. In other situations the male and female decisions are equal. For example, when parents are heirs to their deceased children's estate, both the mother and father receive an equal share of the inheritance. This indicates that the legal ruling is not a matter of men themselves being better or worth twice as much as women. Rather, it takes into consideration a young man's financial obligations to his other family members after his parents are gone.

Islam teaches that this financial obligation to other family members is independent of time and place. It does not matter how much technology a society has, because brothers are responsible for their sisters. This should reduce the drama of inheritors vying with one another for the favor of the soon-to-be-deceased.

Even if a woman makes more money than her husband and brother and father, that money is HERS ALONE to spend on whatever she wishes. She is not required to spend on her own food, clothing, or housing. That is the responsibility of the men around her (father or brother or husband or son). That is her right in Islam. Women are free from this burden so long as they live. If she helps to pay the bills or even if she pays all the bills, that is considered charity from her to her men-folk, and she will be rewarded as such by God. But if a man does not support his elderly parents, his wife, his children, and his unmarried sisters, it is considered a SIN and negligence of his duty to his family.

Islamic inheritance law is one part of a complete system that seeks to institutionalize justice, compassion, and caring in the family, independent of whether women can work for themselves or not. By the way, many Arab women worked or were even business owners during the time of the Prophet. There was Khadijah, the wife of the Prophet; Hind, the wife of Abu Sufyan; Kawlah, the sister of Dirar, and many others. So arguing that this rule "only makes sense in the 7th century" neglects the reality of that time and culture.

You will find almost all the laws that were revealed in Chapter 4 to be tied by this concept. Family is the building block of society. But since not everyone has that natural empathy to love their brother as they love themselves, the Qur'an spelled it out. All peoples, from the north to the south and the east to the west and the past to the future know what are the rights and obligations of each member to another member, and the inheritance laws reinforce the theme of pulling together no matter what the external circumstances, so that no one's rights are trampled. Values, if they are good values, should never go out-of-date; therefore, the protection and care that men are supposed to have toward their women should also never go out-of-date.

(2) Yes, homosexual and lesbian acts are forbidden. However these verses are usually interpreted to mean if a Muslim woman fornicates with a pagan or Muslim man, respectively.

May peace be with you,
Ahmed

Email #20 – From: Winston
Sent: Wednesday, April 6, 2011 7:22 p.m.

Hello Ahmed,

Thank you for responding to my previous questions. I wish to ask you two questions about your last email and one question about a verse in the Qur'an.

(1) You mention, in the previous correspondence, that Muslim men must financially support every member of their family. Is that command based on the verse 4:34? If not, then in what section of the Qur'an is this order stated?

(2) You mention in the previous correspondence that when parents are heirs to their deceased children's estate, both the mother and father receive an equal share of the inheritance. Where in the Qur'an is that command stated?

(3) Regarding verse 4:25, this verse appears to state that women are valued based on income level. In the passage, Allah seems to order that a female maid or housekeeper must receive half the penalty (for committing adultery) than women who are wealthy. If Muslim women receive different punishments depending on income, then this is oppressive. People should not be chastised if they have more money, because wealth is only a tool that can be used to commit evil or good actions. Wealth in and of itself is neither good nor bad. Is there another reason why a maid will get half the penalty?

May peace be with you,
Winston

Email #21 – From: Ahmed Rashed
Sent: Saturday, April 9, 2011 12:30 p.m.

In the Name of God, the Most-Gracious, the Ever-Merciful:

Hello Winston,

Lots of questions this time! That's ok; we'll take the issues one at a time, as before:

Inheritance and Adultery

1. Yes, 4:34 explicitly states that men are the supporters and maintainers of women. This verse was revealed in the context of husbands and wives, but the Prophet and his Companions regularly enjoined men to care for their mothers, aunts, sisters, and daughters who did not have husbands to maintain them. So we see the wisdom behind the choice of words "men" and "women" in general rather than "husbands" and "wives," which is the specific situation that this verse was revealed to address.

2. This rule is in the verse you already mentioned 4:11. The math is there, but it is not apparent until you apply to a test situation. **And there is one-sixth of the inheritance for each of his parents if he has a child, but if he does not have a child and the parents are the heirs then one-third for the mother. (4:11)**

The Arabic word *walad* has been variously translated as child, son, children, and offspring by translators. However, there is universal agreement amongst the Sunni Muslim jurists that *walad* here refers to any child or agnatic grandchild (that means a grandchild through the son).

So if there is a child or agnatic grandchild amongst the heirs, then each of the parents inherits one-sixth. In the absence of a child or agnatic grandchild, the mother inherits one-third; the share of the father is not mentioned under these circumstances. The father in fact inherits as a residuary under these circumstances. Residuary means the heir gets whatever remains of the inheritance after the Qur'anic sharers have been allocated their shares; residuary heirs are generally male agnates.

3. This verse is not talking about "maids" or "housekeepers." It is talking about female slaves. I would blame your English translation for that misunderstanding. That verse is saying that if a man cannot afford the dowry to marry a free woman, then it is better to marry a slave woman (maid) with her owner's permission **"and give them their dower according to what is fair, neither committing fornication nor taking secret paramours."**

If a free woman, whether housekeeper or maid or secretary or doctor or lawyer or whatever, commits fornication, her punishment is one hundred lashes (as described in chapter 24). If it is a slave woman, whether housekeeper or maid or secretary or doctor or lawyer or whatever, commits fornication, her punishment is fifty lashes, half that of the free woman.

The scholars commented on the wisdom behind this distinction:

Al-Qurtubi said: *"The wisdom behind their punishment being less is that they are weaker than the free women, and it is said: they do not get what they want in the same manner as the free women do. It is also said: 'The punishment is determined according to the extent of the favour of Allah upon the person.'"*

At-Taahir Ibn 'Ashoor said: *"Whoever contemplates the Shariah (Islamic Law) will see that there is wisdom behind making the punishment graver according the strength of the betrayal of the person and the weakness of his or her excuse."*

The distinction between the punishment for a free woman vs. the punishment for a slave is similar to the punishment for adultery vs. the punishment for fornication. The fornicator is unmarried, so they are succumbing to temptation when they have no legal outlet for their desires. The adulterer is married, so they are succumbing to temptation when they DO have legal outlet for their desires. For this reason, the punishment of the adulterer is greater than that of the fornicator.

We can discuss this point more, if you wish; or if you are satisfied with these answers we can move on to the rest of the chapter.

May peace be with you,
Ahmed

Email #22 – From: Winston
Sent: Monday, April 11, 2011 10:58 a.m.

Hello Ahmed,
Thank you for responding to my previous questions. Could you please help me to understand the following verses from the Qur'an:

Inheritance and Adultery

(1) Regarding verse 4:19, the passage states that men cannot violate the rights of the widows, of dead relatives, but if these women commit adultery, then men are allowed to violate. Is this an additional punishment for adultery after receiving fifty or hundred lashes?

(2) Regarding verse 4:28, it mentions that human beings were created weak. Weak compared to what or who? If people are weaker than animals, then why do humans dominate over them? Does this verse compare strength of mankind to that of angels or jinns?

May peace be with you,
Winston

Email #23 – From: Ahmed Rashed
Sent: Monday, April 11, 2011 12:00 p.m.

In the Name of God, the Most-Gracious, the Ever-Merciful:
Hello Winston,

Before I respond to these questions, I'd like to know what you thought of my previous responses. Do they make sense? How did they influence or change your initial impressions, if at all?

May peace be with you,
Ahmed

Email #24 – From: Winston
Sent: Wednesday, April 13, 2011 11:34 a.m.

Hello Ahmed,

Your responses to my questions were clear and concise. Muslim men usually inherit more than women because they are required to care for their entire family. The female slaves of Muslims are punished less than free female Muslims because, according to scholars, slaves have less self-control. My first impression of these verses was that Islam oppresses women. I had verified your statements from Islamic websites, reading some fatwas, and listening to some online lectures. I am almost certain that Islam does not oppress women. I say "almost" because I have not read the whole Qur'an, and there are hundreds of fatwas as well as many lectures to explore. Thus, my knowledge of Islam is like a building under construction.

May peace be with you,
Winston

Email #25 – From: Ahmed Rashed
Sent: Friday, April 15, 2011 9:34 a.m.

In the Name of God, the Most-Gracious, the Ever-Merciful:
Hello Winston,

It is so heartening to know that we can make a difference. There is so much negative information out there that it is easy to lose hope that dialogue can clear away the barriers to understanding. Your response really made my day, so I thank you for that. Two minor points from this response before I answer your questions:

a) Criminal punishments for slaves were half of that of free, whether male or female.

b) The scholarly understanding of why half-punishment is wise is the not so much that slaves have less "self-control," but rather that they are more susceptible to compulsion. This does not excuse them of guilt, but rather —as I tried to explain with the fornication/adultery example — it means that they were not fully at liberty to willfully choose to commit the crime.

Now for your questions:

1) No; it is never permissible to violate the rights of widows. The verse says it is illegal to inherit women, period. The conditional clause is referring to holding them in their homes and taking back their dowry. This is usually forbidden, but if the woman is guilty of adultery, then as mentioned in the previous verse, their punishment is confinement to the home, and if the man chooses to divorce her because of her infidelity, then the man is NOT obligated to pay her the deferred dowry, which is usually due to her in case of divorce.

Inheritance and Adultery

This is similar to modern pre-nuptial agreements where the man writes that his wife gets a certain sum of money in case of divorce, except if the divorce is caused by her infidelity.

2) Ibn Abbas, a famous Qur'an scholar who was a Companion of the Prophet, said that this verse specifically refers to weakness of men in the face of temptation from women. We understand this from the context of the previous three verses, which talk about women, seeking marriage, and how those who follow their lusts want believers to stray very far away.

Scholars have confirmed this specific meaning and added the general meaning that mankind is prone to error, sin, and falling to temptation but that God is ever ready to forgive those that sincerely repent to Him. The verse is a response to the idea that any man who sins or falls to temptation or lust is "beyond redemption." Even if a man or woman succumbs to temptation (even adultery), God is ever-forgiving to the sincerely repentant.

I hope this answers your questions adequately; feel free to respond if you have further questions or comments.

May peace be with you,
Ahmed

Email #26 – From: Winston
Sent: Sunday, April 17, 2011 9:13 p.m.

Hello Ahmed,

Thank you for responding to my previous questions. Could you please help me to understand the following verses from the Qur'an:

I am very confused about verse 4:25. Based on your previous emails, are you saying that enslaving a person will make them more tempted to commit adultery because the sin is an expression of freedom? Slaves have no legal outlet for their desire for freedom, because they are restricted from making a lot of personal decisions, but the choice to do what Allah has forbidden is one of the few they can make. Thus they must receive half the punishment instead of the full amount.

Regarding verse 4:47 and 4:154, according to these passages Allah had punished those among the Jewish people who had broken the Sabbath. The fact that Allah chastised people for such an act implies that keeping the Sabbath was a commandment. Based on my understanding of Islam, Allah's commandments are part of his message (the Qur'an). Since the Qur'an that was revealed to the first Prophet (peace be upon him) is the same Qur'an that was received by the last Prophet (peace be upon him), then Muslim must also practice the Sabbath. Do Muslims practice the Sabbath, or do they practice it in a different way than the current Jewish people?

May peace be with you,
Winston

Email #27 – From: Ahmed Rashed
Sent: Monday, April 18, 2011 12:21 p.m.

In the Name of God, the Most-Gracious, the Ever-Merciful:
Hello Winston,

Hopefully, we can clear up Verse 4:25. I did not mean that slaves are more *tempted* to committing adultery. My point is that historically, slaves were more *susceptible* to being coerced into immoral behavior. Unlike free men and women, slaves did not have an extended family or a reputation to worry about. We know this because we have a narration about the conversion of Hind bint Utbah (wife of the chieftain of Quraysh) to Islam. In the narration, the Prophet explains what is expected of her as a Muslim: not to worship anything but God, not to steal, not to commit adultery or fornication, not to kill her children, and not to disobey the Prophet. It is written that she responded with surprise and indignation: *"Does a free woman fornicate!?"*

From this narration, we see how rare it was for free women to commit this act. Remember, Winston, in THAT society at THAT time, when a man wanted to commit adultery or fornication, he would usually seek out a slave girl. This is because it would be a scandal if a free woman (married or not) consented

Inheritance and Adultery

to such an act. Obviously, there were free women and men who did this sin anyway, but the fact remains that this "peer pressure" was not present with slaves (either men or women).

Remember that Islam came to reform, not to revolutionize. This means that radical cultural changes were handled in stages. For example, the rules for widows' inheritances and remarriage came down in two stages. The prohibition of alcohol came down in three stages. The rules for the punishment of adultery also came down in two stages. The first stage (4:15-16) was the "first warning" punishment for this crime. The second and final stage (24:2-3) came down much later, after the Muslim community had a chance to purify itself of this vice. However, the society of the Prophet regularly exploited slaves for sex, this rule is meant to demonstrate the grave status of this vice (even if it is a slave) but at the same time make it more lenient so that the cultural change has time to sink in and become the new norm.

So why wasn't this ruling abrogated as the Muslim community developed? The reason is that there would still be slaves who are "new" to the Muslim community. There are still bad Muslims who would seek to exploit the ignorance of these slaves into doing immorality with them. Slaves outside of the Islamic world had no rights, so new slaves would come under Muslim control assuming the same was true with this new set of masters. This verse ensures that even if a slave didn't realize that slaves are held to the same standards of morality as free, their crime would not be ignored, but at the same time it would take into account their position in society and show them a degree of mercy.

As for the Sabbath, when you get to Chapter 7, you will find more details there. The short answer, however, is that the Sabbath was a specific injunction to a specific people for a specific reason. The specific people were the Children of Israel. The specific reason was to test their faith after they had shown stubbornness before, and they had vowed to God that they would repent and be obedient to His commands. So it is NOT binding on any other community. In fact, one of the things that Jesus came to absolve the Jews from was the Sabbath (see 3:50). The Qur'an was only revealed to the Last Prophet. Every Prophet received a scripture for himself and his community. Some verses are common between the scriptures. Some are not. All verses are in *The Mother of Books*, which is also known as *The Preserved Tablet* in the Qur'an. This tablet is with God, so all scriptures come from the same source, but not all are intended for all communities and all times. The Qur'an is the only scripture to be intended by God to be for all times and all places, and the only scripture to be preserved by God to stay unchanged and uncorrupted.

May peace be with you,
Ahmed

Inheritance and Adultery

With Dialogue Comes Understanding

SCRIPTURE AND DIVINE DECREE

Email #28 – From: Winston
Sent: Tuesday, April 19, 2011 4:02 p.m.

Hello Ahmed,

Thank you for responding to my questions. Could you help me to understand the following verses from the Qur'an:

In your previous email, you mention the following: The Qur'an was only revealed to the Last Prophet. Every prophet received a scripture for himself and his community. Some verses are common between the scriptures. Some are not. If you are saying that each prophet (peace be upon them) received different messages according to particular circumstances, then that appears to contradict a fundamental principle of Islam. This principle is articulated in verse 3:84 of the Qur'an: **"We believe in God and what was revealed to us, and what was revealed to Abraham and Ishmael and Isaac and Jacob and the Tribes, and what was given to Moses and Jesus and to the Prophets from their Lord. We do not separate between them, and to Him we submit."** In order for this passage to be logically correct, the Holy Scriptures revealed in the past (i.e., Tawrat and Injil) must contain the same message that is in the Qur'an. Although there are special rules that are only applicable to a specific community in a specific time period, most of the content in all these books must be the same. If the message is not the equal, then every prophet (peace be upon them) received different instructions from Allah, which results in different religions. Therefore, it does not make sense that the scriptures are based on particular circumstances (i.e., the Prophet himself and his community), because they will no longer be relevant if these circumstances change. The message of Allah must apply to all circumstances. Were you trying to say something else in your last email, and have I misunderstood your words?

Regarding verse 4:78, Allah appears to state that anything good or evil that happens to a person is from Him, but that seems to contradict the passage 4:79. What is the meaning of verse 4:78?

May peace be with you,
Winston

Email #29 – From: Ahmed Rashed
Sent: Friday, April 22, 2011 1:05 p.m.

In the Name of God, the Most-Gracious, the Ever-Merciful:
Hello Winston,

Muslims are required to believe in all the messengers sent by God, without making distinctions among them and without rejecting some messengers while accepting others. The Qur'an says, **Verily, those who disbelieve in God and His messengers and wish to make a distinction between God and His messengers saying, 'We believe in some and reject others' and wish to adopt a way in between, they are in truth disbelievers. And we have prepared for the disbelievers a humiliating punishment. (4:150–151)**

The role of a prophet or messenger is to convey God's guidance and revelations to his people. Because these teachings were often corrupted after the people learned them, a new prophet would be sent to reaffirm the original message. The laws brought by each prophet differed from one another depending on the time and place, because each prophet was sent specifically to his people only. However, the CORE message of all prophets was always, *"O People! God is ONE, and HE commands that you worship NONE but HIM."*

The Qur'an mentions some of prophets sent to the Children of Israel: Moses and Aaron, David and Solomon, John son of Zachariah, and Jesus son of Mary (peace be upon them). To the Arabs, the Qur'an mentions the prophets Hud, Saalih, and of course, Muhammad. To other nations, the Qur'an mentions Idriss, Luqman, and Dhul-Qarnayn. The Qur'an only mentions about twenty-five prophets by name, but Prophet Muhammad (pbuh) taught that over one hundred thousand prophets were sent throughout history to communities around the world. The Qur'an confirms this: **And indeed we have sent Messengers before you; some of them we have related to you their story and some we have not related to you their story. (40:78)**

Muhammad was the last in this line of prophets. He is the "Seal of the Prophets" because there will be no more messengers after him. Unlike previous prophets, the scripture revealed to Muhammad has not been changed or lost; the teachings of Muhammad have been preserved; and laws revealed to Muhammad are for all mankind, not just his people.

So the important point is that previous messengers were only intended for their immediate community. This is why the laws are slightly different, out of God's wisdom and mercy for his diverse creatures. This is also why God did not prevent human tampering. It was part of His plan that these teachings would be lost, forgotten, or corrupted and that new prophets would be sent to correct the deviation of the peoples. These new prophets would confirm the CORE teachings of previous prophets and either confirm, correct, or even change the NON-CORE teachings of previous prophets.

However, Muhammad's teachings and revelation (the Qur'an) was intended by God to be for all people and for all places. For this reason, God promised that He Himself would safeguard this final revelation from human tampering. For this reason, while Muslims believe in the ORIGINAL books revealed to previous prophets, Muslims only follow the teachings of the Qur'an and the Prophet Muhammad.

As for your second question, the answer lies in an intervening word that is in the first verse but not in the second verse. Unfortunately, this is usually not translated. Let us look at the verses as usually found in translation:

Wherever you may be, death will find you, even if you are in fortified towers. If any good befalls them, they say, "This is from God," and if any bad befalls them, they say, "This is from you!" Say, "All is from God;" what is wrong with these people, they barely understand anything said! (4:78)

Any good that befalls you is from God, and any bad that befalls you is from yourself. We have sent you as a messenger to the people and God is enough as a witness. (4:79)

Now let us take the relevant parts of the verse in Arabic with the English directly under:

4:78

qaaluu	hadha	min	ind	Allah
they say	This is	from		God

qaaluu	hadha	min	ind	ik
they say	This is	from		you

Qul	Kullun	min	ind	Allah
Say	All is	from		God

4:79

Ma	asabaka	min	hasanatin	fa	min	Allah
Whatever	happens to you	from	good	so is	from	God

Wa	maa	asabaka	min	sayyiatin	fa	min	nafsik
And	whatever	happens to you	from	evil	so is	from	yourself

Notice that the Arabic word *ind* is found intervening in 78 but not in 79. The word *ind* literally means "with" or "near" or "possessing." For example, the Arabic sentence *Al Malu Ind Ik* means The Money Is With You.

So the first verse is saying that the good and bad results are "with" or "owned" by God, whereas the second verse is saying that those good results are due to God's mercy and bounty, and those bad results are due to your sins and errors.

So we understand these two verses as follows. Everything is under God's control (4:78, 8:17) and bad things happen to us because of our wrong choices (4:79, 42:30, and 64:11). For instance, a person may harm himself by putting his hand in the fire, and the harm is invited by his action, so the result of getting burned is "from you." However, since the fire operates and burns according to God's law, it is "from God." A direct word-for-word translation would be "it is from with God." This obviously has no meaning in English, so most translators do not put it in.

It is noteworthy that the word *ind* in verse 4:78, which indicates intervening causes, does not exist in verse 4:79. In the former, the indirectness of the relationship is implied, whereas in the latter, the directness of the relationship is implied. This is what Muslims mean when they say "the cause of burning is fire, but the CAUSER of burning is God."

May peace be with you,
Ahmed

ON HYPOCRITES

Email #30 – From: Winston
Sent: Saturday, April 23, 2011 1:15 p.m.

Hello Ahmed,

Thank you for responding to my questions. Could you help me to understand the following ayahs from the Qur'an:

(1) Regarding ayah 4:89, the passage appears to mention that hypocrites (that is, anyone who claims to be a Muslim but in reality is not practicing Islam) should be chastised in some way. Are pious Muslims ordered to physically hurt hypocrites, or are they command to ostracize them from society? This ayah seems to contradict 4:63, in which God required Muslims not to trouble hypocrites and even counsel them. According to Islam, how are hypocrites suppose to be treated in society?

(2) Regarding ayah 4:92, it states that blood money is to be paid to the family of a Muslim who has been accidentally murdered by another Muslim. Who determines the amount of money to be paid to the victim's family? Do the two families meet in an Islamic court, and the judge(s) decides the amount of compensation? If Islamic courts generally make these verdicts, then are Muslims required to settle disputes (regarding any legal issue) in Islamic courts (if they exist in the area) instead of the courts of the country they reside in?

May peace be with you,
Winston

Email #31 – From: Ahmed Rashed
Sent: Monday, April 25, 2011 2:54 p.m.

In the Name of God, the Most-Gracious, the Ever-Merciful:
Hello Winston,

(1) The relevant part of the verse is "**Do not take them as your allies until they emigrate in the way of God.**" This is referring to those hypocrites who actually bore arms against the Muslims. They claimed to be believers or allies, but they fought alongside the tribes who were at war with Medina.

That is why the next verse says that if you catch them in the field, they should be treated as enemy combatants. This is further shown by the next two verses:

But make an exception of those who seek refuge with people with whom you have a treaty, or who come over to you because their hearts forbid them to fight against you or against their own people. Had God pleased, He would have given them power over you, so that they would have taken up arms against you. Therefore, if they keep away from you and cease their hostility and propose peace to you, God does not allow you any way against them. (4:90)

This shows that those "hypocrites" who live with a community at peace with Muslim community or those who emigrate away from the enemy people because they *do not want to fight against the Muslim community or their own community* are to be spared the treatment described in 4:89. This is a very clear directive that any people who are not hostile to Muslims or propose peace to the Muslim community are to be left alone and not harmed or attacked in any way.

You will find others who wish to be safe from you, and from their own people, yet whenever they find an opportunity of inflicting harm, they plunge into it. So if they neither withdraw, nor offer you peace, nor restrain themselves from fighting you, seize and kill them wherever you encounter them. Over such people We have given you clear authority. (4:91)

This is the specific kind of hypocrite that this passage is all about: those people who claim to be peaceful but who plunge into conflict against the Muslim community anytime they think the hostile tribe will defeat the Muslim community. This clearly shows that the strong response from the Muslims is only ordained by God against those who refuse to offer peace or stop fighting against the Muslim community. It is these people that God directs Muslims to be tough and strong against so as to protect their lives, families, and homes, and to deter like-minded people from causing mischief against Muslim communities.

So we see that these verses do not refer to people who claim to be Muslims but in fact do not really believe (topic of 4:63); rather, they refer to people who claim to be Muslims and peaceful but in fact are belligerent and continue to fight against Muslim communities and neither withdraw nor offer peace.

(2) The blood money (*diyya*) is dependent on time and place. It is the usual tort penalty for accidental loss of life. In Arabia, this was usually sixty camels. Nowadays, different countries have different standards. The rate is not something that is decided upon between family of victim and perpetrator; rather, it is supposed to be the standard for the land that has jurisdiction over the two.

Muslims are supposed to be law-abiding citizens of whatever country they live in. Islamic law and Islamic courts are the ideal for many devout Muslims, but the current situation means that most Muslims appeal to secular courts, since Islamic courts only have jurisdiction over certain crimes or claims. Saudi Arabia, Iran, and to a lesser extent, Sudan and Pakistan are the only countries in this day and age that have full integration of Islamic law with the government court system.

May peace be with you,
Ahmed

Email #32 – From: Winston
Sent: Tuesday, April 26, 2011 3:18 p.m.

Hello Ahmed,

Thank you for responding to my previous questions. Could you please help me to understand the following ayahs from the Qur'an:

Regarding ayah 4:97, if the angel's task was to take the soul of the unbeliever to hell because he or she did not accept Islam, then why is the unbeliever asked about migrating out of an oppressive country?

Regarding ayah 4:100, if the religion of Islam can be practiced in any part of the world, then why is God commanding people to leave their country in order to become a Muslim?

May peace be with you,
Winston

Email #33 – From: Ahmed Rashed
Sent: Wednesday, April 27, 2011 12:15 p.m.

In the Name of God, Most Gracious, Most Merciful:
Hello Winston,
These verses do not all refer to people who live in a land that does not allow them to practice Islam. If you recall the discussion of jihad was started back in 4:71, and 4:75 points out that it is a communal obligation for Muslims to help and fight for those who are oppressed. So 4:97-100 is talking about people who claim that they did not accept Islam because of the persecution in the land where they live. These verses refute that argument that they will offer; they will be treated like the rest of the disbelievers in that oppressive land. Only those who are truly unable to leave their homes for the sake of being able to worship God will be excused.

These verses were revealed shortly after the Prophet and his companions migrated from Mecca to Medina. This migration was actually MANDATORY on the Muslims at that time because of the harsh persecution the Quraysh were dealing out to anyone who was found out to be a Muslim, but there were a few Muslims who did not migrate. Some did not because they honestly could not make the journey (as mentioned in 4:98), but most because they were not willing to part with their wealth and property. God is rebuking those who sell their faith for worldly comforts. God is also warning that "living in a land of oppression" is no excuse before God as to why a man did not practice the religion that God has prescribed for humanity.

If a Muslim is able to openly proclaim, display, and practice his faith (prayer, fasting, charity, pilgrimage, lifestyle), then he can live in that land. However, if he cannot do these openly, then he is obligated to relocate to a land (any land) where he does have that freedom.

In fact, the whole history of the initial Islamic conquests is actually a response against the great empires that killed or tortured anyone who accepted the religion of Islam. These empires did not allow their subjects to choose a religion other than that of the rulers. Islam mandates that "there is no compulsion in religion," so the Muslims saw themselves as liberators, first and foremost, to allow the population the freedom to accept Islam without fear of retribution, and secondly to secure the population's freedom to stay with their own religion without fear of retribution or injustice.

May peace be with you,
Ahmed

Plural Wives Revisited and Islamic Criminal Law

Email #34 – From: Winston
Sent: Thursday, April 28, 2011 1:00 p.m.

Hello Ahmed,

Thank you for responding to my previous questions. Could you please help me to understand the following ayahs from the Qur'an:

Regarding ayah 4:129, it mentions that a man cannot treat his wives equally, which contradicts 4:3, in which God makes it permissible to have four wives if they are treated the same. What were the circumstances in which the Prophet Muhammad (peace be upon him) revealed verse 4:129?

Regarding ayah 5:33 and 5:38, punishing people that are proven guilty of crimes by killing them or cutting off body parts seems excessive compared to nonviolent methods of punishment (i.e., prison, paying a fee, temporary forced labor, etc.). Furthermore, a nonviolent method of retribution creates the possibility of rehabilitating these people and gives them more time to repent to God. Are violent punishments more common in Islamic law than nonviolent methods? Is the Islamic system of criminal justice very different from the US justice system?

May peace be with you,
Winston

Email #35 – From: Ahmed Rashed
Sent: Monday, May 2, 2011 12:17 p.m.

In the Name of God, Most Gracious, Most Merciful:

Hello Winston,

4:3 refers to time, attention, money, and gifts that a man spends on his wives. Since these are within a man's control, God has mandated the man to be equal and fair.

4:129 refers to the internal feelings of love and fondness. Since these are not within a man's control, God has pardoned whatever inner feelings a man may have so long as he does not leave the other wives "hanging," as mentioned in the verse.

This is similar to the Prophet's sayings regarding a man treating his children fairly; he should give each child equal time, attention, money, and gifts, even if his heart may lean toward one or away from another.

The context of these verses are when the Prophet was considering divorcing one of his wives (Sawdah) because he felt that he could not have the same internal feelings of love and fondness with her as with his other wives. Since 4:3 had already been revealed, the Prophet felt that this meant he was being unjust to her and that he should separate from her. However, Sawdah wanted to remain married to the Prophet, so she offered to give up her nights to Aisha so the Prophet would not divorce her. These verses came to relieve the dilemma of the Prophet's household. First, it said that Sawdah's reconciliation offer is not forbidden. Second, it said that a man's heart can never be perfectly equalized, so the man should accept this reality and **"make amends and act righteously"** among his wives.

These verses were revealed before 33:51-52, which is where God told the Prophet that he could not marry any new wives or divorce any of his current wives. So the issue became a moot point as far as the Prophet was concerned, but these verses are still applicable to Muslims in general who have multiple wives.

As for the punishments prescribed in Islamic law, remember that the primary purpose of punishment is to deter would-be criminals from committing the crime in the first place. Since "an ounce of prevention is better than a pound of cure," the penal system of Islam seeks to prevent crime in the first place.

On the surface, the deterrent punishments in Islam appear to be harsh, but it is only meant for such incorrigible offenders who stand as real obstacles to the healthy growth of human society. In fact, it was a vital instrument in building a new social order, and it radically reformed the pre-Islamic system where inhumanity and unchecked vengeance was the order of the day. Prisons in Western societies are miserably failing its people, and apart from being living hell, prison destabilizes people and often has a destructive effect on the personality. Home Office statistics in Britain show that longer sentences do not prevent reconviction; in fact, 50% of males and 35% of females are convicted within two years after coming out of prison. So if the laws of punishment do not fulfill the main objective of making a safer society, it is not true to say that prison is the more appropriate punishment for theft rather than the amputating of a hand. If reducing the crime rate is the objective, then certainly the choice will be the Islamic criminal justice system — you just have to compare the crime statistics of Saudi Arabia or any Gulf country to any American state of comparable population and judge which one is better at fulfilling that objective.

May peace be with you,
Ahmed Rashed

INTERFAITH FRIENDSHIPS AND THE STATUS OF JEWS IN ISLAM

Interfaith Friendships and the Status of Jews in Islam

Email #36 – From: Winston
Sent: Tuesday, May 3, 2011 4:44 p.m.

Hello Ahmed,

Thank you for responding to my previous questions. Could you please help me to understand the following ayahs from the Qur'an:

Regarding ayah 5:51, since there are Muslims who live in countries where the majority of people do not practice Islam, then it becomes necessary to make friends with that majority. In order to function in society, a person needs to build relationships of mutual respect with others because each individual has something the other wants. All human beings exchange different objects and services with each other depending on their circumstances. If Muslim communities isolate themselves in Christian and Jewish nations, it will be very hard for those communities to prosper. Why does God appear to order His followers not to befriend Jewish people and Christians?

Regarding ayah 5:64 and 5:82, one of these passages addresses the Jewish people as immoral and the other as possessing hatred of Muslims. Most of the ayahs (in the second, third, four surahs) that refer to the Jewish people consist of very strong criticism. These condemnations are usually limited to either a few among them or a majority. However, there are some verses such as 2:96 in which God appears to criticize the entire Jewish community. The ayahs of 5:64 and 5:82 seem also to address the whole population. If these sections of the Qur'an were limited to a specific time, that means the children of Israel had become completely corrupt several times in history. Is that why God continue sent one Prophet (peace be upon him) after another to the Jewish people, to bring a majority or a few back to the path of Islam? If these verses were not limited to a specific time and since no human being can be born wicked, then there is something intrinsic in the Jewish religion that encourages individuals to be depraved. That is the only conclusion can be derived without these limitations. If that is the meaning of these ayahs, it appears that Islam is antisemitic. The definition of antisemitism is a dislike or hatred for Jewish people. Hatred for any group is justified only if they are iniquitous, because people who have little or no virtue are a threat to everyone. Therefore, characterizing the Jewish religion as being unethical, to some degree, will automatically result in people loathing them. In other words, these verses appear to be indirect commands to hate the Jewish people. What were the circumstances in which the Prophet Muhammad (peace be upon him) revealed these verses?

May peace be with you,
Winston

Email #37 – From: Ahmed Rashed
Sent: Wednesday, May 4, 2011 2:04 p.m.

In the Name of God, Most Gracious, Most Merciful:

Hello Winston,

Islam teaches us that we should be friendly to all people. Islam teaches us that we should deal even with our enemies with justice and fairness. The Qur'an says in the beginning of the same Surat Al-Ma'dah: **O you who believe! Stand out firmly for God as witnesses to fair dealings and let not the hatred of others to you make you swerve to wrong and depart from justice. Be just, that is next to piety. Fear God, indeed God is well-acquainted with all that you do. (5:8)**

In another place, the Qur'an says: **God does not forbid you, regarding those who have not fought you in religion's cause, nor expelled you from your homes, that you should be kindly to them, and act justly towards them; surely God loves the just. God only forbids you as to those who have fought you in religion's cause, and expelled you from your homes, and have supported in your expulsion, that you should take them for allies. And whosoever takes them for allies, those are the evildoers. (60:8-9)**

Moreover, God Almighty has described Prophet Muhammad (peace and blessings be upon him) as "a mercy to the worlds." He was a sign of God's mercy to all, Muslims as well as non-Muslims. In his kindness and fair treatment, he did not make any difference between the believers and nonbelievers. He was kind to the pagans of Mecca and fought them only when they fought him. He made treaties with the Jews of Medina and honored the treaties until they broke them.

He (peace and blessings be upon him) is reported to have received the Christians of Najran with kindness in his Masjid in Medina. They argued with him about Islam, but he returned them with honor and respect. There are many examples from his life that show that he was the friendliest person to all people.

In the verse you quoted (5:51), the word *"Awliya"* is used. It is the plural of *"wali,"* and the correct translation of the word *"wali"* is **not** *"friend."* Rather, it refers to a very close and intimate *ally, protector, patron, close relative,* or *master*.

In the Qur'an, the word *"wali"* is used for God, in His capacity as *Protector*: **God is the *Wali* of those who believe. He takes them out from the depths of darkness to light; (2:257)**

Also in the Qur'an, the word *"wali"* is used for a human being, in their capacity as *close relatives*: **And whosoever is killed unjustly, We have granted his *wali* the authority to seek judgement; (17:33)**

Therefore, the correct translation of the verse in Surat Al-Ma'idah is: **O you who believe! Do not take Jews and Christians as your *patrons*. They are *patrons* of their own people. He among you who will turn to them for *patronage* is one of them. Verily God guides not the unjust people. (5:51)**

It is obvious that Jews patronize other Jews, and Christians patronize other Christians, so why is it strange that Muslims patronize other Muslims and support their own people? Let us look more closely at the context and history of this verse. In his Qur'an commentary, Imam Ibn Kathir has mentioned that some scholars say that this verse (i.e., the one you referred to) was revealed after the Battle of Uhud, when Muslims suffered a loss. At that time, a Muslim from Medina said, "I am going to live with Jews so I shall be safe in case another attack comes on Medina."

And another person said, "I am going to live with Christians so I shall be safe in case another attack comes on Medina." So God revealed this verse reminding the believers that they should not seek the protection from others, but should protect each other. (See Ibn Kathir, Al-Tafsir, vol. 2, p. 68)

Muslims are allowed to have non-Muslims as friends as long as they are able to keep their own faith and commitment to Islam pure and strong. You are correct in pointing out that a Muslim man is also allowed to marry a Jewish or Christian woman. It is obvious that one marries someone for love and friendship. If friendship between Muslims and Jews or between Muslims and Christians was forbidden, why would Islam allow a Muslim man to marry a Jew or Christian woman? That does not make any sense. The verse is merely teaching that Muslims should not patronize anyone who is against their faith or who fights their faith, even if they were their fathers and brothers. The Qur'an says: **O you who believe! Take not your fathers and your brothers as *awliya* if they love unbelief above faith. If any of you do so, they are indeed wrong-doers. (9:23)**

However, if some Muslims do wrong to some non-Muslims, it is Muslims' duty to help the non-Muslims and save them from oppression. The Prophet (peace and blessings be upon him) said that he himself will defend a non-Muslim living among Muslims to whom injustice is done by Muslims.

As for the Qur'anic description of the Jewish people, please remember that the Old Testament also contains strong criticism of the Jews. The reason for both is that the people who witnessed a prophet (whether Muhammad, or Jesus, or David, or Samuel, or Isaiah, etc.) had become far astray from the teachings of the Divine Revelation.

You are correct that the Children of Israel had gone astray many, many times, and so this is why God send them many, many prophets, for the purpose of bringing them back to the straight path. Remember verse 3:113-114, **"Not all are alike..."** Also remember 3:199, **"And there are certainly among the People of the Book..."**

So the Qur'an does not deny that there is good in the Jewish community. Rather it calls out those who stray from the original teachings of the prophets and who deny and disbelieve in a new prophet who has just appeared to them.

What happened to Muhammad from the Jewish community of his time (denial, disbelief, and fighting against him) is the SAME thing that happened to Jesus and David. This is why these two Prophets are mentioned in the same passage. Even after these verses were revealed and after the battles between the Muslim community and some tribes of the Jewish community, the peaceful, nonbelligerent Jews and Christians were allowed to live and practice their faiths in peace.

The only reason why the Qur'an is so critical of the Jews in general is because if they truly wished to adhere to their Torah as they claimed, they would have accepted the new prophet that God had sent. For example, when David was made a prophet, some refused to follow him, claiming they would only follow what Moses brought. Were these true believers? The whole reason why God sent David was to correct the waywardness that had crept into the scripture and practice of the Jews since that time. Likewise, when Jesus was sent to "the lost lambs of Israel," some refused to follow him because they claimed they would only follow what Moses and David had brought. Once again, this section of the Jews missed the whole point. Jesus was sent because the Jews had strayed from those earlier teachings. Those that followed Jesus came back to the correct path of God and can truly be called believers. Finally, when Muhammad was sent, many refused to follow, while some did accept Muhammad as the promised Last Prophet that was in their own books.

Ibn Sallam, a Jewish rabbi, was one of the first to accept Muhammad. Makhriq, a rich Jewish noble, also accepted Muhammad and even fought and died in the Battle of Uhud. So again, remember 3:113-114: **"They are not all alike...**

May peace be with you,
Ahmed

Email #38 – From: Winston
Sent: Saturday, May 7, 2011 7:02 a.m.

Hello Ahmed,

Thank you for responding to my previous questions. However, you did not completely answer my second question. I know that Islam is not antisemitic. The English translations of ayahs 2:97, 5:64, and 5:82 are very disturbing because they appear to be antisemitic statements for the reasons I had described in my previous email. What is the meaning of these verses in the classical Arabic? Do these ayahs refer to specific time periods in history? What were the circumstances in which the Prophet Muhammad (peace be upon him) revealed these verses? What lessons is God teaching Muslims in these verses?

May peace be with you,
Winston

Email #39 – From: Ahmed Rashed
Sent: Tuesday, May 10, 2011 1:02 p.m.

In the Name of God, Most Gracious, Most Merciful:

Hello Winston,

Regarding 2:97, let us first look at the historical context of this chapter. The greater part of Al-Baqarah was revealed during the first two years of the Prophet's life at Medina. At Mecca, the Qur'an generally addressed the pagan Quraysh, who were ignorant of Islam, but at Medina, it was also concerned with the Jews who were acquainted with the creed of the Unity of God, Prophethood, Revelation, the Hereafter, and angels. They also professed to believe in the law, which was revealed by God to their Prophet Moses (pbuh), and in principle, their way was the same that was being taught by Prophet Muhammad (pbuh).

In [2:40–120], invitation to the Guidance has particularly been extended to the Children of Israel, and their past and present attitude has been criticized to show that the cause of their degradation was their deviation from God's guidance.

Interfaith Friendships and the Status of Jews in Islam

The Jews have been exhorted to follow Prophet Muhammad (pbuh) who had come with the same guidance and who was a descendant and follower of Prophet Abraham whom they highly honored as their ancestor, and professed to follow as a prophet. The verse in question is actually a part of God's sermon to the Children of Israel to stop their rebelliousness and follow the prophet who had been sent to them.

Here is the complete passage, which is called *"Learning from the History of the Israelites"* by some scholars:

When they are told, "You shall believe in these revelations of GOD," they say, "We believe only in what was sent down to us." Thus, they disbelieve in subsequent revelations, even if it is the truth from their Lord, and even though it confirms what they have! Say, "Why then did you kill GOD's Prophets, if you were believers?"

Moses went to you with profound miracles, yet you worshipped the calf in his absence, and you turned wicked. We made a covenant with you, as we raised Mount Sinai above you, saying, "You shall uphold the commandments we have given you, strongly, and listen." They said, "We hear, but we disobey." Their hearts became filled with adoration for the calf, due to their disbelief. Say, "Miserable indeed is what your faith dictates upon you, if you do have any faith."

Say, "If the abode of the Hereafter is reserved by GOD for you, to the exclusion of all other people, then you should long for death, if you are truthful."

They never long for it, because of what their hands have sent forth. GOD is fully aware of the wicked. In fact, you will find them the most covetous of life; even more so than the idol worshipers. The one of them wishes to live a thousand years. But this will not spare him any retribution, no matter how long he lives. GOD sees everything they do.

Say, "Anyone who opposes Gabriel should know that he has brought down this [Qur'an] into your heart, in accordance with GOD's will, confirming previous scriptures, and providing guidance and good news for the believers." Anyone who opposes GOD, and His angels, and His messengers, and Gabriel and Michael, should know that GOD opposes the disbelievers.

We have sent down to you such clear revelations, and only the wicked will reject them. Is it not a fact that when they make a covenant and pledge to keep it, some of them always disregard it? In fact, most of them do not believe. Now that a messenger from GOD has come to them, and even though he proves and confirms their own scripture, some followers of the scripture disregard GOD's scripture behind their backs, as if they never had any scripture. (2:91-101)

Now that we have the entire passage, let us break it down section by section and explain its context:

[2:91-93] is an introduction to the Children of Israel and the actions that caused that community to lose God's blessings. It is understood that those individuals who held fast to God's commandments are **exempt** from this criticism.

[2:94-96] was a retort that implied that if they really were sure and enamored of the Hereafter, they would not dread death, but would prefer it to the life in this world. They, however, were so much given to this worldliness that they were terrified by the very thought of death and the Hereafter. "They" refers to the Jews who argued with Muhammad and denied his Prophethood, not to the entire Jewish community.

In [2:96], the literal translation of the phrase *"ala hayatin"* is "any kind of life." It means that they wished to live without giving any consideration to the kind of life they led. It did not matter whether that was a life of honor and grace, or a life of dishonor and disgrace.

[2:97-98] responds to the fact that the Jews of Medina not only reviled Muhammad (peace be upon him) and the believers, but also spoke abusively of Gabriel, the chosen Angel of Revelation. They said. "He is our enemy: He is not an angel of blessings but of affliction."

[2:99-101] conclude the passage with a divine commentary to the Prophet to not be disheartened by their rejections and ridicule. In other words, God is consoling Muhammad that while most of the Jews refuse to follow him, this is due to their sins and not their nature. [2:99] says **"only the wicked."** [2:100] says **"most do not believe."** [2:101] says **"some followers of the scripture..."**

Regarding 5:64 and 5:82, we again look at the historical context of this chapter. It was revealed after the treaty of Hudaibiyah at the end of 6 A.H. or in the beginning of 7 A.H. That is why it deals with those problems that arose from this treaty. Since almost all habitations in north Arabia had come under the rule of the Muslims, the focus shifted from security to inviting people to the faith. The Jews especially have been warned again about their wrong attitude and invited to follow the Right Way. This is because Jews lived in Arabia, especially in and around Medina. Although they initially swore friendship and peace with Muhammad, they later taunted and mocked him, charging him with ignorance. They also began to plot with Muhammad's enemies in Mecca to overthrow him (despite having signed a peace treaty). After each major battle, Muhammad accused one of the Jewish tribes of treachery and attacked it. These incidents were not religiously motivated; they were politically motivated. The remaining Jewish tribes (Bani Harith, Jusham, Najjar, Sa'ida, Shutayba, and Quda'a) continued to live in Arabia unmolested, and they were able to continue their farming, trade, religious lives, and family lives. Even in Medina itself, individual Jews who stayed aloof from the treacherous acts of the "big three" tribes were allowed to continue their livelihood.

Specifically, about 5:64, according to the Arabic idiom, *"one whose hands are chained"* is an excessively stingy person. What the Jews of the seventh century Arabia meant by this was that God had ceased to be bounteous. They used to lament their lost glory and blame God for being miserly toward them. So again this is a response to the words and attitudes of SOME of the Jews of Medina.

As for 5:82, this is merely a divine statement of fact. The vast majority of converts to Islam are former Christians. Very few Jews (or pagans, for that matter) accept Islam or even bother to initiate or even engage in any interfaith dialogue or community service. However, for over fourteen centuries, this kind of dialogue and common service to the poor has been a staple of Muslim-Christian relations. In the past, this has been between individuals; in modern times, this has been between whole congregations and even leaders of congregations.

In conclusion, these passages reproach the Jews of seventh century Medina for their refusal to recognize Muhammad as a Prophet of God. But this reproach is only against the Jews who lived in Muhammad's time and met and witnessed Muhammad first-hand. While it is true that these verses can be interpreted as general condemnations, due to the Qur'an's timely process of storytelling, the majority of scholars agree that all references to Jews or other groups within the Qur'an refer only to specific populations at specific points in history. Remember, the Qur'an also says: **Those who believe, and the Jews, and the Sabi'un, and the Christians, who believe in God and the Last Day and do good, there is no fear for them, nor shall they grieve. (5:69)**

So we see that the criticisms deal mainly with the transgressors and irreverent among the Jews of Muhammad's time. Generalizations to previous and later generations of Jews are only valid inasmuch as these other generations of Jews act as the Jews of Muhammad's time acted.

Muhammad's disputes with his neighboring Jewish tribes left no marked traces on his immediate successors (known as Caliphs). The first caliphs based their treatment upon the Qur'anic verses encouraging tolerance. Classical commentators viewed Muhammad's struggle with Jews as a minor episode in his career, but this has changed in modern times due to the fallout from the creation of the State of Israel at the expense of the indigenous Palestinians.

May peace be with you,
Ahmed

With Dialogue Comes Understanding

On Sacrifices and Sleeping Souls

Email #40 – From: Winston
Sent: Wednesday, May 11, 2011 5:28 p.m.

Hello Ahmed,

Thank you for responding to my previous questions. Could you please help me to understand the following ayahs from the Qur'an:

Regarding ayah 5:97, sacrificial offerings and consecrated cattle are mention in this verse. Are these sacrificial offerings specific animals or could they be any halal animal? Are cattle the only animals to consecrated, or can there be others? How does an animal become consecrated?

Regarding ayah 6:60, it appears that God is stating that when people sleep they die and when they awake, they are resurrected. If that is true, then where does a person's soul go when people are sleeping? If the spirit does not leave the body, then how is it that we are dead when asleep?

May peace be with you,
Winston

Email #41 – From: Ahmed Rashed
Sent: Friday, May 13, 2011 6:25 p.m.

In the Name of God, Most Gracious, Most Merciful:
Hello Winston,

(1) For Hajj or Umrah, a pilgrim may slaughter a goat or sheep, or seven pilgrims can share in the slaughter of a cow, buffalo, or camel.

(2) Souls are taken up to God's care during sleep or unconsciousness but not completely (as in death), which is why the sleeper still shows signs of life.

Below are some commentaries of the scholars on this issue (but God alone knows best):

It was narrated that Hudhayfah ibn al-Yamaan said: When the Prophet (peace and blessings of God be upon him) went to bed, he would say: *"In Your name I live and die,"* and when he got up he would say: *"Praise be to God Who has given us life after taking it from us and unto Him is the Resurrection."*

Al-Nawawi said:

What is meant by (taking away from us) is sleep. The Prophet (peace and blessings of God be upon him) pointed out that waking up after sleep which is like death is an affirmation of the resurrection after death. The scholars said: The wisdom behind saying the du'aa' when wanting to sleep is so that a person's final deed will be this du'aa', and the wisdom behind saying the du'aa' when waking up is so that the first of his actions will be remembrance of Tawheed and good words.

Ibn Taymiyah said:

Here God explains that the taking away of souls is of two types:

He takes them away at the time of death, and He takes away the souls that did not die in their sleep. Then when they sleep, he keeps the soul of the one who dies in his sleep and He sends back the soul of the one who did not die in his sleep. Hence when the Prophet (peace and blessings of God be upon him) went to bed, he would say, "In Your name my Lord I lie down and in Your name I rise, so if You should take my soul then have mercy upon it, and if you should return it then protect it in the manner You protect Your righteous slaves."

Ibn al-Qayyim said:

Sleep is the 'lesser death.' In sleep, the soul comes out and travels until it comes into the presence of the Lord of the Throne. If the sleeper is in a state of purity, his soul prostrates before its Creator. Then it may encounter the world of dreams or meet with souls of people who have died, but what it is in fact faced with is a page of God's knowledge of the Unseen containing the good or evil he has decreed for this particular human being. If the sleeper is truthful, generous, and pure, then when his soul returns to him, it conveys to his heart the truth of what God has let him see (a truthful dream).

In sleep, the soul can also move freely about the world and meet with souls of people who are still alive and gain knowledge from them. Some of what it learns is true and some false. The false part is the normal dream or the chatter of the soul.

If the sleeper is a untruthful and likes what is false, his soul still rises to the heaven during sleep, moves freely about the world, meets other souls and learns true information about the unseen. However while the soul is returning to the body, it meets Shaytan in mid-air and he mixes the true with the false. Then when he wakes up, the person is confused about what God has let him see and consequently does not understand it (a confused dream).

In the sleeping state, the soul does not completely leave the body as it does in the case of death, but remains inside the body not leaving it to move freely through the heavens. We can liken it to a ray or thread whose end remains connected to the body.

May peace be with you,
Ahmed

PROPHET IBRAHIM AND THE FUTURE OF ISLAM

Email #42 – From: Winston
Sent: Sunday, May 15, 2011 7:37 p.m.

Hello Ahmed,

Thank you for responding to my previous questions. Could you please help me to understand the following ayahs from the Qur'an:

Regarding ayah 6:75, did Ibrahim (peace be upon him) became a Muslim after seeing the visible and invisible worlds? If Ibrahim (peace be upon him) gained Iman (faith) without witnessing miracles, then what were the circumstances or the event in which he (peace be upon him) became a believer?

Regarding ayah 6:116, does the verse apply only to a specific time period? If the ayah is addressed to every future generation, then that would mean Islam will never become the religion for a majority of people. If Islam were to become the largest religion in the world, then this verse would be a contradiction.

May peace be with you,
Winston

Email #43 – From: Ahmed Rashed
Sent: Tuesday, May 17, 2011 12:34 p.m.

In the Name of God, Most Gracious, Most Merciful:

Hello Winston,

Ibrahim (pbuh) was a natural monotheist, like all the other prophets. His heart and nature were in tune with the signs all around him that there IS a creator and that this creator must be ONE and TRANSCENDENT. The story related in this passage (verses 74-82) are about how he pondered one night and translated this intuition into a rational argument. This rational argument both solidified his faith and provided grounding to confront his polytheistic community.

Ayah 6:116 was revealed specifically to address the Prophet's arguments with pagans around him. It is also applicable to all later generations, as the Prophet prophesied, *"Islam began as something strange and it will end as something strange, so Glad Tidings to the strangers!"* The point is that the right thing for a truth-seeker is not to consider what way the majority of the people are following, because that is based on guesswork instead of knowledge. Their beliefs, theories, philosophies, principles of life and laws are the result of guesswork and are, therefore, sure to mislead. In contrast to that, the way of life with which God is pleased can only be the Way that God Himself has taught. Therefore, the seeker-after-truth should adopt that way and steadfastly follow it, even though he is left alone on it.

The Prophet also was instructed in the Qur'an that most people will NOT believe. You will read verses that imply this meaning in several chapters as you go thru the Qur'an. This is true at any instant in time, and it is definitely true for all mankind cumulatively. The Prophet compared righteous believers and wicked disbelievers like the head of a man who is beginning to gray; most hairs are black (evil), a few are white (good), and several are in various stages of gray (in between).

Note that the issue is not Muslim vs. non-Muslim *per se*, but rather it is about those who are on the right guidance and right behavior. Many, many Muslims in this age, as in previous ages, do bad things, so their label of Muslim does not make them automatically "rightly guided."

May peace be with you,
Ahmed

With Dialogue Comes Understanding

The Jinn, the Devil, and Paradise

Email #44 – From: Winston
Sent: Wednesday, May 18, 2011 11:04 a.m.

Hello Ahmed,

Thank you for responding to my questions. Could you help me to understand the following ayahs from the Qur'an:

Regarding ayah 6:130, it appears that the jinns had their own apostles. Do the Qur'an or the Prophet Muhammad (peace be upon him) mention the names of these apostles? Did the jinns receive their own version of the Qur'an? What kind of life do jinns live, and can you describe their civilization?

Regarding ayah 7:26, what does that dress look like? Can you send me a picture of the clothing? Is there a male and female version? Are all Muslims required to wear it at all times, or only in the public areas?

May peace be with you,
Winston

Email #45 – From: Ahmed Rashed
Sent: Monday, May 23, 2011 12:25 p.m.

In the Name of God, Most Gracious, Most Merciful:

Hello Winston,

The jinn are part of the unseen world. As such, we only know about them what God revealed to Muhammad in the form of either Qur'an or Hadith.

From 6:130, we know that God has sent prophets and messengers to jinn from within the jinn community. However, neither the Qur'an nor any Hadith mention jinni prophets or scriptures.

From 46:29-32 and all of chapter 72, we know that some jinn are Jews (following Moses) and some are Christian (following Jesus), and many are wicked disbelievers who follow Satan. These passages also imply that Muhammad was sent as the final messenger to both jinn and humans. This implication is confirmed by an explicit Hadith of the Prophet.

From various Hadith of the Prophet, we know that jinn can be either good or evil, and that they are born, grow old, marry, have children, eat, drink, and die. We know that they are stronger and faster than humans, with the ability to fly. We know that they do NOT know the secrets of the unseen, but rather they must eavesdrop on angelic or human conversations to learn anything new. We also know they are not as intellectual or technological as humans (they do not invent things or investigate the nature of the universe like humans do).

As for 7:26-27, there is no specific dress to which to refer. Let us read the text of this passage and the scholarly interpretation:

O children of Adam, We have sent down to you clothing in order to cover the shameful parts of your body, and to serve as protection and decoration; and the best garment is the garment of piety. This is one of the signs of God; it may be the people learn a lesson from this.

O children of Adam, let not Satan seduce you in the same way that he caused your first parents to be driven out of the Garden and stripped them of their garments in order to expose their shameful parts before each other. He and his party see you from where you cannot see them. We have made these satans the guardians of those who do not believe.

Here is the explanation of this passage according to the late Sayyid Abul Ala Maududi:

In this passage, the Qur'an has used the story of Adam and Eve for the eradication of the evil of nakedness. Satan had seduced the Arabs of the pre-Islamic period into believing that clothing was meant merely for the purpose of decorating and protecting the body from the hardships of weather. Accordingly they totally disregarded its real purpose and paid no heed to cover their shameful parts and did not hesitate to uncover them before others in the open. Above all, they would go round the Ka'abah in perfect nudity during the Haj season; and their women were even more shameless than their men. That was because they considered it a religious act and did this as if it were a virtuous deed.

The whole human race has been addressed because this evil was not confined to the Arabs alone but many people of the world had been (and even today are) guilty of this. Therefore the whole human race has been warned, as if to say, "O children of Adam! Nudity is a clear manifestation of the fact that you have been seduced by Satan. As you have discarded the Guidance of your Lord, and rejected the Message of His Prophets, you have given yourselves up to Satan who has misled you from the way of natural modesty into that shameful state, in which he intended to mislead your first parents. If you consider it seriously, you will come to the inevitable conclusion that you can neither understand rightly the demands of your nature nor fulfill them without the Guidance of the Messengers."

This passage brings out the following facts about clothing:

(1) The need of clothing has not been artificially created in man, but it is an important urge of human nature. That is why God has not created a natural covering for the human body, as He has done in the case of all other animals. Instead, He has instilled inherently the feelings of modesty and shyness in human nature. Besides this, He has not made his sex organs as merely sex organs, but has also made them shameful organs, which, by his very nature, he does not like to expose before others. Moreover, He has not given man any ready-made covering for hiding the shameful parts, but has ingrained in the human nature that man should hide them with clothing. This is what v. 26 implies. God has inspired man with the urge to hide the shameful parts of the body. Therefore man should understand the nature of this inspired urge and make clothing for himself from the material provided by Him.

(2) The fact that in v. 26 the covering of the shameful parts precedes the protecting and decorating of the body, is a clear proof that more importance has been attached to the moral than the physical function of clothing. Thus it is obvious that the human nature is quite different from the animal nature. That is why Nature has made provision for the protection and decoration of the body of the animals, but has ingrained no urge in them for the covering of their shameful parts. But when the human beings discarded the Guidance of God and began to follow the guidance of Satan, they reversed the above order as if to say, "Your clothing is merely to protect and decorate your bodies just as the

skins cover the bodies of the animals. As regards the covering of the shameful parts, garments have absolutely no importance, for these are merely sex organs and not shameful organs."

(3) The garments should not only be the means of covering the shameful parts and of protection and decoration but should also enable man to attain piety. The dress should, therefore, be such as to conceal those parts of the body that should be hidden from others; it should neither be too expensive nor too poor with regard to the position of the wearers; it should not smack of haughtiness nor arrogance nor hypocrisy. Moreover, the garment of piety demands that the male should not wear the female dress and vice versa, and that the Muslims should not imitate blindly the non-Muslims in dress. It is obvious that only those who believe in the Guidance of God and follow it can attain the desired standard of the garment of piety. But those who discard the Guidance of God and make satans their guides, are misled by them into one error or the other in regard to clothing.

(4) Clothing is one of God's many signs which are spread all over the world and which lead men to the recognition of the reality, provided that one sincerely seeks it. If one seriously considers the above-mentioned three facts about clothing, one can easily understand how clothing is an important Sign of God.

The Prophet Muhammad instructed his followers what the practical fulfillment of this passage should be, and that way has been handed down generation to generation as the Islamic dress code. Islam enjoins a modest dress code for men and women who are not married to each other. For both sexes, the clothing must not be see-through and must not be tight in a way that reveals the shape or figure of what is covered.

For men, they must cover from the belly button to the knees. This is the dress code for men in front of their family and other men. If a man goes out where unrelated women can see him or wishes to say his obligatory prayers, he must cover his shoulders in addition. This is the minimum amount of clothing that is considered decent for a man; more clothing would be considered more modest. Obviously, a man's wife can see as much of her husband as she wishes without sin on either party.

For women, they must cover from the shoulders to the knees. This is the dress code for women in front of their family and other women. If a woman goes out where unrelated men can see her or wishes to say her obligatory prayers, she must cover her entire body except for her face and hands. This is the minimum amount of clothing that is considered decent for a woman. Obviously, a woman's husband can see as much of his wife as he wishes without sin on either party.

May peace be with you,
Ahmed

Faith, Reason, and the Nature of Adam

Email #46 – From: Winston
Sent: Tuesday, May 24, 2011 6:24 p.m.

Hello Ahmed,

Thank you for responding to my previous questions. Could you please help me to understand the following ayahs of the Qur'an.

Regarding ayah 7:11–25, God discusses how He created two human beings and placed them in paradise, and these people were allowed everything except the fruit from a tree. Iblis beguiled them into eating the fruit, and God punished the first humans by sending them to live on Earth. That is the origin of mankind, according to Islam, but over the past two hundred years people have developed a theory of our origin based on observation and testing. There is an enormous amount of biological and archeological evident that demonstrates that people evolve from simpler organisms that evolve from ever more simpler creatures in a lineage spanning about a billion years. Since there is an apparent contradiction between scientific knowledge and the revealed knowledge, then the following question needs to be asked. **Does God wish to make it impossible to prove with objective evidence that all the supernatural events in the Qur'an actually occurred?** The Prophet Muhammad (peace be upon him) seems to emphasize that faith should not require proof in the following authentic Hadith:

Narrated Abu Huraira: The Prophet (peace be upon him) said: *"There was no Prophet among the Prophets but was given miracles because of which people had belief, but what I have been given is the Divine Revelation which God has revealed to me. So I hope that my followers will be more than those of any other Prophet on the Day of Resurrection."* (Hadith No. 379, Vol. No. 9, Sahih Al-Bukhari)

If the last Prophet (peace be upon him) expected his followers to have faith that is not supported by evidence, such as performing miracles, then that appears to imply that God will not allow anything to exist that can objectively prove these extraordinary events in the Qur'an. I am not a Muslim, so it is possible that I am making false assumptions about this Hadith and ayahs 7:11–25. However, it seems to me that the consequence of having an objective way of verifying these miracles is that there will be no struggle to obey God. In other words, the inner jihad would not exist. If the physical proof was discovered, then individuals will convert to Islam in order to adapt to circumstances, just as an animal adapts to the weather in order to survive. This decision becomes necessary if there is evidence that guarantees success in this world and in an afterlife. Any decision that is optional, by definition, would become a struggle to perform, because there is no evidence that guarantees success. Therefore, evidence of faith contradicts a struggle to have faith.

May peace be with you,
Winston

Email #47 – From: Ahmed Rashed
Sent: Monday, May 30, 2011 5:09 a.m.

In the Name of God, Most Gracious, Most Merciful:
Hello Winston,

First let me apologize for taking so long to get back to you. Work was very hectic last week due to the end-of-month deadlines.

The short answer to your question is "no."

As many Muslim intellectuals have stated, "Reason is the pioneer of faith." This means that Islam considers the intellect and critical observation to be tools that the unbiased observer will use to come to the realization of God's existence and the inevitable return to Him. However, it also warns that only those whose hearts are not polluted by love of this worldly life or by arrogance will have the clarity of vision to correctly conclude the greatness of God from these external observations.

The Qur'an specifically says, **We shall show them Our signs in the horizons and within themselves, until it becomes clear to them that this is the Truth. Is it not enough that your Lord is the witness of all things? Yet they still doubt that they** will ever meet their Lord. Surely, He encompasses all things. (41:53-54)

Also, the Qur'an encourages and even commands man to explore the world and see how God's handiwork has been carried out: **Do they not see how God originates creation, then reproduces it? That surely is easy for God. Tell them, "Roam the earth and see how He originated creation. Then God will bring into being our second life. God has power over all things." (29:19-20)**

In Islam, physical nature is pointed out as the great divine manifestation, and Islam firmly believes that the working of physical nature shows enough signs of rationality, method, and adaptation for goodness, to give a knowledge of God to those who apply their reason without any narrow, preconceived notions or bias. The Qur'an calls itself the book of wisdom, and it never asks us to believe without giving a careful rationale of that belief. No other scripture commands its readers to "look", "think," and "learn" like the Qur'an. It is for this reason that many Muslims and non-Muslims say that this empirical attitude that infused the first Companions of the Prophet heralded the scientific age of reason and applied intellect.

Islam and the Qur'an have never had a problem with science and empirical investigation. There are many verses in the Qur'an that are amazing for their compatibility with modern science, despite the fact that the Qur'an was revealed over fourteen centuries ago. That is the meaning of the Hadith you quoted. Other Prophets had miracles that had to be witnessed first-hand in order to convince their people. The Last Prophet had a miracle that only requires one to approach the book with an open and discerning mind. Having said all this, inner jihad will still exist because God is subtle, and only those whose hearts and minds are seeking God will find Him. The Qur'an mentions that when the disbelievers see the angels and the major signs of their Lord, their repentance will not be accepted; the reason for this is because it will then be a matter of fact, not a matter of faith.

As for evolution, Muslims are generally agreed (though

there are some exceptions) that the Qur'an does not preclude the idea that animals evolved from one form to another. One of God's Names is *Al-Bari*, which means the Maker. This is contrasted with His Name *Al-Khaliq*, which means the Creator. *Khaliq* refers to His ability to create something from nothing. *Bari* refers to His ability to make something from something else. Since God is considered the causer of causes, the laws of gravity, electromagnetism, chemistry, and even biology are all seen as manifestations of His Will, Power, and Knowledge. In Islam, none of these forces are seen as "independent" or "autonomous" from God; rather they are seen as manifestations of God's Will and Actions.

However, the origin of man is still under debate in Islamic scholarly circles. The majority believe that the Qur'an teaches an explicitly special creation. That means that Adam had no ancestor, no father, and no mother. So this interpretation is in contradiction to current evolutionary theory. They use the following verses to justify their stance: **Jesus in the sight of God is like Adam. He created him from dust; then said to him, 'Be!' and he was. This is the truth from your Lord, so do not be among the doubters. (3:59-60)**

There is a growing minority who argue that "creation from the earth" could be interpreted in the evolutionary sense. They use the following verses to justify their stance: **What is the matter with you that you deny the greatness of God, when He has created you through different stages? (71:13-14)**

[Do you not see] how God has produced you from the earth and caused you to grow, and how He will then return you to it and bring you forth again? (71:17-18)

To explain Adam's special relationship to God, they use the following verse: **Your Lord said to the angels, 'I am about to bring into being a man wrought from mud. When I have formed him and** *breathed My spirit into him*, **fall down in prostration before him,' (15:28-29)**

So instead of interpreting that Adam had no father or mother, they interpret that Adam did have physical ancestors, but that he was the first proto-human that God "**breathed His spirit**

into him." So in a sense, this spiritual birth marks Adam as something unique in the world: physically connected to the earth but spiritually connected to the heavens.

I hope this answered your question. Feel free to reply if you would like to discuss this issue further before you continue to read through the Qur'an.

May peace be with you,
Ahmed

Email #48 – From: Winston
Sent: Wednesday, June 1, 2011 10:40 a.m.

Hello Ahmed,

Thank you for responding to my previous questions. Could you please help me to understand the following ayahs from the Qur'an:

(1) Regarding ayah 7:11, were Adam (peace be upon him) and his spouse biologically the same as you and me when they resided in Jannah and on Earth? For example, did they have the same physical appearance, lifespan, susceptible to illness, etc.?

(2) Regarding ayah 7:19 and 7:22, in the first verse God mentions that eating fruit from a certain tree will make Adam (peace be upon him) and his spouse immoral. Does that imply that before Adam (pbuh) performed this act, he (pbuh) was not capable of being iniquitous? Did the fruit of that tree itself make Adam (pbuh) wicked, or was it the fact that he (pbuh) disobeyed God's command? In verse 7:22, it is mentioned that Adam (pbuh) and his spouse felt ashamed of their nudity immediately after eating the fruit of the forbidden tree. Shame is a characteristic behavior of someone possessing Islamic morals, because in ayah 7:26, God commands Adam (pbuh) and his spouse to wear clothing to hide their nakedness. Thus, there appears to be a contradiction. God prohibits people from eating the fruit of that tree because it will make them unethical, but the fruit itself has given people knowledge of ethics that God confirms to be correct in the Qur'an. If God's moral laws, based on the Qur'an and

Sunnah of Prophet Muhammad (pbuh), only apply on Earth and not on Jannah, then there is no contradiction. If God created a different ethical standard for Jannah, then is that the reason why Adam (pbuh) and his spouse never felt ashamed of their nudity before eating the forbidden fruit?

May peace be with you,
Winston

Email #49 – From: Ahmed Rashed
Sent: Wednesday, June 8, 2011 1:19 p.m.

In the Name of God, Most Gracious, Most Merciful:

Hello Winston,

Please forgive the long delay; work is very hectic this month.

To proceed:

1. Most scholars say there is a difference between them living in Eden and living on Earth. In Eden, they were very tall, and they did not get sick. According to some scholars, they did not display any of the lower body functions (gas, urine, stool, spit, mucus, and the like). Other than that, they looked like modern humans. However, when they disobeyed God, this is when "**their shame was made apparent to them.**" Some scholars say this means not only that they noticed they were naked, but they actually started excreting waste (gas, urine, stool, spit, mucus, and the like) as a result of their disobedience. When they came to Earth, they obviously continued to display lower body functions, and they were reduced in stature to what most humans are today. The Prophet is reported to have said that Adam and the early generations were tall and long-lived and that each successive generation had both reduced height and lifespan until the height and lifespan of current humans was reached.

2. Adam and Eve knew right from wrong, ethics and morals, from the day they were "awakened." Both had the knowledge of right from wrong and the ability to choose right or wrong from the beginning. The fruit itself had no power or

significance. It was merely a test of their obedience to God. Satan tempted them by TELLING them it would give them knowledge and power (according to the Bible), or it would make them angels and immortal (according to the Qur'an). Satan was a liar; it was the disobedience that made Adam and Eve aware of their shame, not any special knowledge imparted by the fruit.

As for different ethical standards between Eden and Earth, God does not operate that way. He is *Al-Barr* (The Good) and *Al-Haqq* (The Truth). He is the absolute standard for morality, ethics, and goodness. The forbidding of the fruit was merely a test, in that all other fruits were lawful. Also remember from chapter 2 that God informed the angels even before creating man that he was going to place him "on Earth." So the descent to Earth was already a part of His plan. As for why Adam and Eve didn't notice they were naked until they disobeyed, as I mentioned above, some scholars say this was because of the physical results that appeared after their transgression. Others say that it was the normal feelings of guilt that come when a human commits a deed that he knows is wrong or against God; however, being the first humans, these feelings of self- and God-consciousness were stronger in them than in us.

May peace be with you,
Ahmed

The People of *A'raf* and the Previous Arabs

Email #50 – From: Winston
Sent: Saturday, June 11, 2011 9:27 a.m.

Hello Ahmed,

Thank you for responding to my previous questions. Could you please help me to understand the following ayahs from the Qur'an:

(1) Regarding ayah 7:46-47, are these verses metaphorical or literal? Who are the men of *al-A'raf*? What is the meaning of a wall between Jannah and hell? What is the meaning of having a veil between the inmates of Jannah and hell when there is already a wall separating them?

There will be a veil between them, and on the wall will be the men of *al-A'raf* who will recognize everyone by their distinguishing marks, and will call to the inmates of Paradise: "Peace on you," without having entered it themselves though hoping to do so. When their eyes fall on the inmates of Hell they will say: "O Lord, do not place us in the crowd of the vile." (7:46-47)

(2) Regarding ayah 7:55, it mentions that Muslims should pray unseen. If Muslims are suppose to perform Salat privately, then why do they pray in large groups in a mosque?

May peace be with you,
Winston

Email #51 – From: Ahmed Rashed
Sent: Thursday, June 16, 2011 2:52 p.m.

In the Name of God, Most Gracious, Most Merciful:

Hello Winston,

Verses 46-47 are literal. What you have translated as "the wall" is actually in Arabic "*al-a'raf*," which means the Heights. So it is not quite right that there is both a "wall" and a "veil" and a "barrier." There is no wall, there is just the Heights; and only God knows exactly how this is. The veil is the barrier, and it will be strong enough to separate Hell and Paradise, but it will not isolate them. The people on "the Heights" will be those with pending cases. While their good deeds will not be so much as to merit admission into Paradise, their bad deeds will not be so much as to condemn them to Hell. Therefore, they will wait for the decisions of their cases on "the Heights" between Paradise and Hell. The scholars have interpreted these verses in different ways. Some say these are people who never received a messenger in their life on Earth. So their test of faith happens on the Day of Judgment, and that is why they are not immediately put in either Paradise or Hell. Some say that these are people whose good deeds and bad deeds are equal, so their case is not immediately clear where they should go.

The meaning of the *hijab* or *barzakh* (veil or barrier) between Paradise and Hell is that the inmates of each will be separated from each other but not totally isolated from each other. Scholars deduce from this dialogue between the inmates of Paradise and the inmates of Hell and the people on "the Heights" that the faculties of men will be stronger in the next world. The faculty of sight will become so strong that the people of Paradise and those of Hell and on "the Heights" will be able to see one another whenever they desire to do so. Likewise, their faculties of speech and hearing will grow so strong that the people of the three different worlds will be able to carry on their dialogues without any hindrance. From this and the like descriptions of the next world in the Qur'an, we learn that the laws of life in the hereafter will be quite different from the physical laws of this world, though there will be no change in our personalities.

As for 7:55, the word in Arabic is *dua*, not *salah*. Remember that *salah* is the formal ritual prayer that is done either alone or in congregation in mosques. *Dua* is simply supplication or calling upon God, so this verse means that Muslims should do their personal supplications privately and with humility. The emphasis is on the humility, not the secrecy.

May peace be with you,
Ahmed

The People of A'raf and the Previous Arabs

Email #52 – From: Winston
Sent: Saturday, June 18, 2011 9:27 a.m.

Hello Ahmed,
Thank you for responding to my previous questions. Could you please help me to understand the following ayahs from the Qur'an:

(1) Regarding ayah 7:65, I had read the Qur'an up to As-Saffat (Surah 37), which is more than half the book. God always describes the Prophet Hud (peace be upon him) and the people of 'Ad in a vague way. Is there any more information in the remaining Surahs of the Qur'an or in the Hadith of the Prophet Muhammad (pbuh) about Hud (pbuh) and his efforts to being his people into Islam? What was Hud's (pbuh) personal life? What is the history, culture, and location of the people of 'Ad?

(2) Regarding ayah 7:73, I had read the Qur'an up to As-Saffat (Surah 37), which is more than half the book. God always describes the Prophet Saleh (pbuh) and the people of Thamud in a vague way. Is there any more information in the remaining Surahs of the Qur'an or in the Hadith of the Prophet Muhammad (pbuh) about Saleh (pbuh) and his efforts to being his people into Islam? What was Saleh's (pbuh) personal life? What is the history, culture, and location of the people of Thamud?

May peace be with you,
Winston

Email #53 – From: Ahmed Rashed
Sent: Thursday, June 23, 2011 1:04 p.m.

In the Name of God, Most Gracious, Most Merciful:
Hello Winston,
The Qur'an is unique in that it only reveals details that are relevant to its message. That is, details about culture or history are only included when they further the goals of making mankind aware of the Rights of God, the Rights of Man, and the consequences of fulfilling or neglecting those rights. So, often the

stories of previous nations are parables that drive home the point of "see what happens to people who reject their messenger," but they do not detail the way of life of those people except in general terms. For this reason, we have only a few details about Hud and Saleh, their personalities, lives, and so on.

As for the people of Ad and Thamud, we do know from the Prophet that Ad were in southern Arabia and Thamud were in northern Arabia. The Prophet passed by the Well of Saleh on his way to Tabuk. He ordered his army not to drink of its water or to make ablution with it. The following link compiles all information from Qur'an, Hadith, and archaeology to describe the people of 'Ad and their descendants Thamud, respectively:

http://www.harunyahya.com/pernat14.php
http://www.harunyahya.com/pernat15.php
May peace be with you,
Ahmed

With Dialogue Comes Understanding

THE SABBATH AND ISLAMIC ASCETICISM

The Sabbath and Islamic Asceticism

Email #54 – From: Winston
Sent: Tuesday, June 28, 2011 11:05 a.m.

Hello Ahmed,

Thank you for responding to my previous questions. Could you please help me to understand the following ayahs from the Qur'an:

(1) Regarding ayahs 7:163-168, God discusses how He tested the Jewish people by requiring them to maintain the Sabbath while, at the same time, tempting them to break it. When the majority of the Jews failed to maintain the Sabbath, God gave them two punishments. Is ayah 7:167 the reason why the Jewish people had been oppressed by various nations for thousands of years (i.e., the nation of Germany killing six million Jews during the 1940s)?

(2) Regarding ayah 8:1, it mentions that the spoils of war belong to both God and the Prophet Muhammad (peace be upon him). However according ayah 8:10, God is the only cause of a military victory. Why are the benefits of a military victory being dedicated to the Messenger (pbuh) in addition to God? Furthermore, this Surah contains several ayahs that command Muslims to obey to both God and His Prophet (pbuh), instead of only God, such as ayahs 7:20, 7:27, and 7:46. All these ayahs give the appearance that the Prophet Muhammad (pbuh) is a partner of God and not simply His messenger (pbuh). Do the words and actions of Prophet (pbuh) represent God's Will? If not, then what is the appropriate relationship a Muslim should have with the Messenger (pbuh)? If Muslims give the Prophet (pbuh) too much respect (like the Christians did to the Prophet 'Isa [pbuh]), that would be attributing partners to God, and if too little respect (as in the cartoons of Muhammad [pbuh] in the Danish newspaper), it would be offensive to God? For example, would the act of celebrating the Prophet's (pbuh) birthday be an act of worshiping Him (pbuh)?

May peace be with you,
Winston

Email #55 – From: Ahmed Rashed
Sent: Monday, July 4, 2011 5:06 p.m.

In the Name of God, Most Gracious, Most Merciful:
Hello Winston,

(1) The two punishments mentioned are for those who actually broke the Sabbath and for those who did not condemn the Sabbath-breakers. If you read the story closely, you will see there are three groups of people: those who sinned; those who did not sin but also did not admonish their brethren; and those who did not sin and called their brethren to stop their sinning by reminding them to Fear God. The non-sinners who did admonishment were saved. The other two groups received differing grades of punishment.

From this, the scholars understand that the duty of enjoining good and forbidding evil a communal obligation. Those who fail to do so will be punished with the sinners if and when God's punishment falls.

For any people (not just Jews), when some members of that people sin, they become liable to God's wrath and punishment. But since God is the *Forbearing* and the *Patient* and the *Clement*, He does not send down his wrath right away. He waits so that the sinners have a chance to repent and the non-sinners around them have a chance to admonish them. If the sinners repent, then no punishment will descend (as God wills). If the sinners do not repent, but their neighbors admonish them, then IF punishment descends (as God wills), the punishment will fall only on the sinners themselves. If the sinners do not repent, and their neighbors do not admonish them, then IF punishment descends (as God wills), then the punishment will fall on the whole community. This is referred in the Qur'an as "Sunnat Allah" or "The Way of God," so this is God's standard operating procedure when it comes to dealing with sinners in society.

The reason for this is that as mentioned in chapters 2 and 7, humans were created to be God's stewards or vicegerents. Therefore, humans are expected to practice stewardship with respect to the earth beneath them, the animals subjected under them, and to the other humans around them. So we see the stories of the previous prophets show that those who followed the Prophet were saved from God's punishment. Everyone else in the society was punished, the active disbelievers and the passive or apathetic disbelievers.

So getting back to your original question, the situation of the Jewish people over the centuries is not seen as punishment for one particular sin in the past, but rather for their continuous sinning in the present. This is also how Islamic scholars explain the sorry status of the Muslim community in this day and age. So long as a society is far from God's teachings and does not enjoin the good or forbid the evil (regardless of what religion that society claims to be), God's Grace and Blessings will not go to it; rather, He will make life hard and toilsome. On the other hand, if a community follows God's teachings, especially His command to establish Justice, then His Grace and Blessings will go to it, and it will be protected from the hostility of its enemies.

(2) So there is one concept that will answer all the questions in this point: Muhammad is the Messenger of God. That means that God authorized and deputized Muhammad to execute God's Will on this Earth. Therefore, as was said in Chapter 4: Whosoever obeys the Messenger has obeyed God. For this reason, this chapter emphasizes that obedience to the Messenger is obligatory, just as it is to the Lord of the Worlds. So why this emphasis now in this chapter? This is because this chapter was revealed right after the first major military victory of the believers over the disbelievers. After the Battle of Badr, the Muslims were obviously elated that God granted them victory against the odds (317 lightly armored Muslims vs. about 1,000 heavily armed and armored pagans), but they also started fighting among themselves over who should get the spoils of war.

This whole chapter was revealed to "get the troops back in line." The first verse is a reference to the fact that the Muslims were not fighting for any worldly benefit; rather, they were fighting for God and that His faith should be strong and defended. Therefore, it is unseemly that when the devotees of God are given victory from Him, they should argue over the worldly glitter. So the spoils are for God.

However, what is to be done with the spoils? God's Messenger is to distribute according to God's command (to be found partially in this chapter and more detailed in chapter 9). This is not to mean that Muhammad is somehow God's "partner" or "associate" (God forbid such a sinful idea!). Rather, just as Jesus and Moses said before, "The way to the Lord is through me." So all decisions, even mundane monetary ones, have to be made according to the sayings of the Prophet (peace be upon him). So the spoils are for God's Messenger, because he is the one authorized by God to distribute to those God has commanded to receive: one fifth to the poor and needy and the common defense and the rest to all soldiers who participated in the battle (regardless of whether they saw action or not or whether they were part of the offense or defense).

The words and actions of the Prophet are not seen as "representing God's Will" as such, but rather the Prophet was given freedom to say and do as he felt appropriate, and "what he felt appropriate" was inspired by God (see 53:3-4). Now, for those very few cases when what Muhammad felt was appropriate did not meet with God's approval, verses were revealed to correct the Prophet (see 9:43, 66:1, and 80:1-10). This is why whenever the Prophet was asked a question about something related to religion, he would be silent for a while, and then when the Angel inspired in him what was God's Will, he would say it in his own words. Sometimes, the response would be important enough that actual verses would be revealed instead of just divine guidance and information. This by the way is one of the proofs that Muslims have that the Qur'an and the religion of Islam did not just spring out of Muhammad's head. These admonitions from God show that Muhammad was not in control of the revelation and that sometimes what he thought was appropriate had to be corrected.

If Muslims give "too much" respect to the Prophet, that would be an act of making partners with God, which is the biggest sin in Islam. If Muslims give "too little" respect to the Prophet, that would be disrespecting God's beloved. Celebrating the Prophet's birthday is seen as inappropriate by conservative Muslims and some moderate Muslims, not because he does not deserve to celebrated or that celebrating is "too respectful," but rather because the Prophet and his companions never did such celebrations. It is known that the Companions loved the Prophet more than any later generation could, so they would have been the first to celebrate his birthday if such a thing was permissible.

And God knows best.

May peace be with you,

Ahmed

Email #56 – From: Winston
Sent: Wednesday, July 6, 2011 10:54 a.m.

Hello Ahmed,

Thank you for responding to my previous questions. Could you please help me to understand the following ayahs from the Qur'an:

(1) Regarding ayah 8:28, it mentions that a person's possessions and children are a temptation to commit sin. In order to avoid those sins, one must reject worldly pleasures as much as possible. Throughout the Qur'an, God commands Muslims to live a modest lifestyle, such as in verses 17:26–27. However, there is a difference between modesty and asceticism. The practice of asceticism requires renouncing worldly pleasures for spiritually and thus doing only what is absolutely necessary to survive. Ayah 8:28 is one of many, such as 33:28–29, that appear to enjoin an ascetic lifestyle. Furthermore, the Prophet Muhammad (peace be upon him) appears to teach his (pbuh) asceticism according to the thirty-first Hadith of Al-Nawawi Forty Hadiths:

Abu-A;-'Abbas, Sahl-Bin-Sa'd Al-Sa'idi, may God be pleased with him, said, "A man came to the Prophet, may God's peace and blessings be upon him, and said, 'Oh, God's Messenger! Show me something that if I do it, God will love me and people will love me.' He replied, 'Be ascetic in life, God will love you. And be sparing in what people have, people will love you.'" [Ibn-Majah]

Does Islam require its adherents to lead a modest life or to become ascetics? Or can a Muslim choose to be an ascetic, but it is not a requirement?

(2) Regarding ayah 8:71, it mentions that the captives of war had deceived God before. How is it possible to mislead God, especially if one of His ninety-nine names is the All-Knowing? What is the meaning of this ayah in the classical Arabic and its context?

May peace be with you,
Winston

Email #57 – From: Ahmed Rashed
Sent: Wednesday, July 6, 2011 12:28 p.m.

In the Name of God, the Lord of Mercy, the Ever Merciful:

Hello Winston,

(1) The Prophet, his Companions, and the Scholars after them teach that there is a difference between having the worldly life in your hand and in your heart. In Islam, all love — which is based in the heart — must begin and end with God.

So family, wealth, and so on are all loved for the sake of God and not for their own sakes. So if a member of your family reminds you of God and does their duty to God, you will love him. If he fights against you because of your faith or is a persistent transgressor and causes corruption and evil in the land or in your life, you will treat him with the respect that God obligates us to treat him with, but you will not love him. Likewise, if your wealth is a means of living and doing good deeds (whether in the form of donations or helping others or advancing the cause of Islam), then it is good. But if it becomes an end to itself, then it is bad.

This is what it means to have the worldly life in your HANDS but not in your HEART. The evil is when God is "partnered" with worldly pleasures in the heart. This is almost idolatrous and blameworthy in Islam. However, if God is the one and only thing that is beloved in your HEART, and your family are beloved to you only because they are in God's path, and your wealth beloved to you only because you use it to stay alive and to do good deeds, then the worldly life is in your HANDS to use and enjoy as long as you do not transgress the limits set by the Prophet and God in your HEART.

Many of the Prophet's companions were successful merchants, and the Prophet never said anything to them about leaving their business or living poorly. In fact, he said, *"God loves to see the results of His bounty upon His servants."* This means that if God gives you good health, you should take care of that health and not hide it. If God gives you children, you should take care of your children and not denigrate them. If God gives you wealth, you should live according to those means that he has bestowed upon you.

However, this is usually not the problem with people; the usual issue is that people see material wealth as the be-all and end-all of existence. This is what is condemned.

(2) Betraying God means disbelieving in Him or worshiping something other than him. This is the primary sin that the pagans of Arabia committed. They ignored all the blessings that God showered upon them and instead worshiped idols of stone and wood. The point is that if there is Good in them, God knows it and will cause it to manifest in the form of their accepting Islam. This actually happened to several prisoners. The secondary point is the Prophet and his companions saying that if you fear that they will continue to fight against you after being released, then do not be afraid, because God already knows who will do so, and He has already decreed that you (the Muslims) will have power of them.

And God knows best.
May peace be with you,
Ahmed

Email #58 – From: Winston
Sent: Monday, July 11, 2011 5:56 p.m.

Hello Ahmed,

Thank you for responding to my previous questions. I have some inquiries about your response to my first question in the last email.

Your explanation of asceticism in Islam seems to only be a metaphor used to describe an Islamic concept. This metaphor ("…in your hand and in your heart…") is used to illustrate that the intention of a pious Muslim should only be to obey God and nothing else. In other words, every action a Muslim performs should be to please God. If that is the message you were trying to articulate to me in your most recent email, then are you saying that the practice of asceticism, which is to physically renounce the pleasures of life for spiritual reasons, in not encouraged by Islam? That would appear to contradict part of the life of the Prophet Muhammad (peace be upon him) because the Prophet (pbuh) used to journey to Mount Hira and climbed up to a cave for spiritual reasons. If the Messenger (pbuh) felt it was necessary to go on several of these spiritual retreats to a desolate cave on a mountain, and if all Muslims are required to emulate the Prophet (pbuh), then Islam does promote some form of ascetic practice. Are Muslims allowed to practice asceticism for a limited amount of time? Throughout the Qur'an, God appears to make a distinction between Islam and the life of this world and demands people to chose one but not both. Such as ayah 57:20, in which God seems to emphatically condemn what the world has to offer (the nonessential aspect) and describes it as insignificant. How can asceticism be simply a metaphor, which was the impression I got from your last email, if God so strongly denounces the pleasures of this life?

May peace be with you,
Winston

Email #59 – From: Ahmed Rashed
Sent: Saturday, July 16, 2011 10:12 p.m.

In the Name of God, the Lord of Mercy, the Most Merciful:
Hello Winston,

I will try to explain more clearly with verses from the Qur'an, Traditions from the Prophet, sayings of the Companions, writings of the Scholars, and commentaries of the Activists.

The Qur'an says:

The true servants of the Gracious One are those who walk upon the earth with humility and ... They are those who are neither extravagant nor stingy, but keep a balance between the two; (25:63-67)

His people said to him, 'Do not exult in your riches, for God does not love the exultant. 77 But seek the Home of the Hereafter by means of that which God has bestowed on you; do not forget to take your share in this world.' (28:76-77)

The Prophet said:

"There is no celibacy in Islam."

"There is no monasticism in Islam."

"Nine portions of God's bounty are in commerce."

"Abstinence from the world is not by denouncing as prohibited that which is permitted or by neglecting wealth to go to waste. On the contrary, abstinence means that you do not place greater reliance on what you have in your own hands than you do on what lies in God's hands, and when misfortune strikes, you have such faith in the reward for bearing it with patience that you wish it could remain with you."

When the Prophet knew of a man who spent all his days in the mosque, praying and reciting Qur'an, he asked the Companions, *"How does he provide for his food and shelter?"* They told him, "His brother spends on him so he can devote all his time to God alone." The Prophet said, *"His brother is better than him."*

The Companion Ali ibn Abi Talib said:

"Detachment is not that you should own nothing, but that nothing should own you."

Imam Hassan al-Basri said:

"Zuhd [detachment from the world] resides in the heart, and it can be achieved by ridding the heart of the slavery from the love and the eagerness for this life. This way, the world will be in one's hand, not in his heart, where the love for God Glorified and Exalted and the Hereafter will and should reside."

Imam Ahmed ibn Hanbal said:

"Zuhd [renouncing worldly pleasures for gaining God's closeness] in this world is: to not be overjoyed with what one possessed and to not be distressed by turning away from it (i.e. the world).

So he (Imam Ahmed) was asked about a man who has 1,000 dirhams, and if such could be considered a zaa'hid (i.e., one who renounces this world).

Imam Ahmed said, "Yes, but with one condition, which is: if his wealth increases, he does not become too joyful; and if it decreases, he does not become distressed."

Imam Ibn Taymiyyah said:

"Zuhd [detachment from the world] is to leave alone those things which will not benefit you in the next life. And piety is to leave the things you fear might harm you in the next life."

"The position of wealth should be regarded like that of the toilet, in that there is need for it, but it has no place in the heart, and it is resorted to when needed."

More recently, Ahmed Taleb of Algeria said:

"The Prophet himself did not opt to live far away from the camp of men. He did not say to youth: 'Sell what you have and follow me.' On the contrary, he worked and toiled among things as they are. He did not achieve the glory of the just, except by way of the risk of his life... We see him sharing personally in the construction of the mosque and the dwellings of the emigrants. Later, carrying arms, he put himself at the head of his troops. Charged to deliver a message, he opted for action, because he was convinced that a message can only pass from the realm of idea to the realm of life by taking the hard road of involvement. Thus, Islam commends action — we plainly see — just as, no less explicitly, it condemns craven aloofness from it."

Finally, Ali Muzrui of Kenya reflected:

"*Commercial activity is ... part of the origins of Islam ... Muhammad might well be the only founder of a major religion who was once a man of commerce. He attended to some of the trading interests of his wealthy wife... A verse from the Qur'an assures Muslims that it is not wrong to seek a livelihood in trade and exchange [even] in the course of the pilgrimage.*"

So this is the orthodox view, but why so much emphasis on renouncing the world in the first place? Why does God so strongly denounce the pleasures of this life? Let me share with you one passage and one Tradition:

But you prefer the life of this world, although the Hereafter is better and more lasting. (88:16-17)

So the reason for the emphasis is that most people prefer the life of this world, even though the hereafter is better and more lasting. This meaning is confirmed by the Prophet's LAST WORDS as he was dying:

"*By God, I do not fear poverty for you; rather I fear that you will covet this worldly life as those before you coveted it, and you will compete over it as those before you competed over it, and it would destroy you as those before were destroyed.*"

So the worldly life is BAD when it is seen as an end of itself. However, it is GOOD when it is seen as tool and gift from God to be harnessed and used for the realization of justice on Earth and the fulfillment of those responsibilities which God has enjoined on humanity.

One more thing, the Prophet never went back to Hiraa after receiving the first revelation. This is the cue to him and all his followers that salvation is not found by running away from the world; it is found by engaging the world and working to make it a reflection of God's Kingdom. This can only be done with effort, resources, wealth, and right guidance.

May peace be with you,
Ahmed

The Verse of the Sword

The Verse of the Sword

Email #60 – From: Winston
Sent: Monday, July 25, 2011 9:49 a.m.

Hello Ahmed,

Thank you for responding to my previous questions. Could you please help me to understand the following ayahs from the Qur'an:

(1) Regarding surah nine, there is no statement "In the name of God, the most benevolent, ever merciful" and no first ayah. Why has God negligent to mention the statement and a verse in this Surah?

(2) Regarding ayahs 9:2–6, is God commanding an Islamic state to conduct a foreign policy, which is the following: First, make a treaty with idolatrous nations and if they maintain the terms of the treaty then peaceful coexistence is possible. Second, if these nations refuse to make a treaty or violate the terms of the agreement, then Muslims must go to war with them until they submit to an Islamic state. Third, an Islamic state should cease warfare during four specific months of year. Is this the meaning of these ayahs? Why do Muslims cease warfare during those four months?

May peace be with you,
Winston

Email #61 – From: Ahmed Rashed
Sent: Friday, July 29, 2011 9:52 a.m.

In the Name of God, the Lord of Mercy, the Most Merciful:

Hello Winston,

(1) There are many opinions among the scholars as to why there is no "Basmalah" at the beginning of this chapter. Some say that it is because of the very stern tone at the beginning. Some say that it is an indication of God's anger at the pagans who continuously broke their covenants. Others say that it is because chapters 9 and 8 were one chapter, not two. These are all opinions. The essence of the matter, however is that there is no "Basmalah"

because it was not included in the official standard Qur'ans that Uthman ibn Affan (3rd Caliph) commissioned. He did not include it in the official standard Qur'ans because the Companions did not recite "Basmalah" at the beginning of this chapter. They did not recite it, because the Prophet did not recite it. And God knows best.

(2) There are two important assumptions which have to be clarified regarding these verses. The first assumption (which I admit even a few Islamic scholars have made) is that these verses represent GENERAL instructions rather than SPECIFIC instructions in a specific context. The second assumption is that the purpose of this fighting is to impose Islamic rule. Both assumptions are not correct. So the "foreign policy," as you describe it, was only commanded for the Companions of the Prophet against their immediate enemies who were continually plotting against the nascent Muslim nation. However, it is NOT a general commandment on how all future Muslim nation-states should act *vis-à-vis* their non-Muslim neighbors.

Sheikh Hânî al-Jubayr, former judge of the Jeddah Supreme Court of Saudi Arabia, has said the following:

If the non-Muslim country did not attack the Muslim one nor mobilize itself to prevent the practice and spread of Islam, nor transgress against mosques, nor work to oppress the Muslim people in their right to profess their faith and decry unbelief, then it is not for the Muslim country to attack that country. Jihad of a military nature was only permitted to help Muslims defend their religion and remove oppression from the people. The Persians and Romans did in fact start aggression against Islam and attack the Muslims first. The Chosroe of Persia had gone so far as to order his commander in Yemen specifically to kill the Prophet (peace be upon him). The Romans mobilized their forces to fight the Prophet (peace be upon him), and the Muslims confronted them in the Battles of Mu'tah and Tabûk during the Prophet's lifetime.

The early Muslims lived in a time when the default status of countries was to be "at war" until there was a formal "peace treaty." We now live in a world where the default status is to be "at peace" until there is a "declaration of war." It is not Islam that

The Verse of the Sword

was spread by violence; rather it is the Muslim empire that spread this way. What I mean is that we must not confuse the political expansion of the Arabs with the religious expansion of Islam. The political powers of the time lived by maxim "conquer or be conquered," and the Muslim polity lived the same way. They were playing the same "Great Game" as the rest of the civilizations around them.

The Qur'an clearly says: **God does not forbid you to have friendly, mutually respectful relations with those who have not attacked you because of your religion and have not turned you out of your homes. God simply forbids you to take as your patrons those who attack you because of your religion or turn you out of your homes or conspire with others to turn you out of your homes. (60:6-8)**

The Qur'anic injunction to fight was clearly connected with the very specific necessity of preserving the physical integrity of the Muslim community at a time and place when fighting, sometimes preemptively, sometimes defensively, was understood to be the only way to do so. Peace, i.e., the repelling of aggression, rather than conversion to Islam, was the ultimate aim of this fighting. This is clearly indicated by several verses, such as [2:193], [8:61], and very bluntly in [4:89-90].

The first thirty-seven verses of this chapter were all revealed just before Hajj in the 9th year of Hijra (one year before the Prophet died), when Abu Bakr had left for Mecca as leader of the pilgrims to the Ka'bah. Therefore, the Companions said to the Prophet, "Send it to Abu Bakr so that he may proclaim it on the occasion of Hajj." He replied, *"The importance and nature of the Declaration demands that this should be proclaimed on my behalf by someone from my own family."* Accordingly, he entrusted this duty to Ali and instructed him to proclaim it openly before the pilgrims, and also make these four announcements: (1) "No one who rejects Islam shall enter Paradise. (2) No pagan should perform Hajj after this year. (3) It is forbidden to move round the Ka`bah in a naked state. (4) The terms of the treaties which are still in force (i.e., with those who have not broken their treaties with the Messenger of God up to that time) would be faithfully observed until the expiry of the term of the treaties."

Verse 9:29 is referring to the Jews of Khaybar and beyond who continued to conspire against the nascent Islamic community. The Christians of Najran were never attacked or even threatened, because they came to terms with the Prophet before any hostility could even develop. Since there were no conspiracies coming out of their quarter, the Muslims never advanced upon them. However, the Jews of Khaybar, the Christians of Byzantium, and the Christians and Zoroastrians of Persia certainly DID make and execute plans to devour the new political power in Medina, so the Muslims were instructed to use force or the threat of force to impose a peaceful stance from their belligerent neighbors.

As for the injunction to abstain from fighting for four months, it is not, as you wrote, a general, four-month-per-year abstention from fighting. Rather, it is just a four-month grace period from the time of announcement to all pagan tribes who had not kept true to their treaties.

May peace be with you,
Ahmed

Email #62 – From: Winston
Sent: Monday, August 8, 2011 5:22 p.m.

Hello Ahmed,

Thank you for responding to my previous questions. Could you please help me to understand the following ayahs from the Qur'an:

Regarding ayah 9:23, it appears that God is commanding Muslims to sever all relations with family members who do not practice Islam. If these non-Muslim family members need help or economically depend on the Muslim member of the family, then abandoning them will hurt them. Is God requiring believers to completely break off all relations with members of their kin because they have a different religion?

Regarding ayah 9:36, God mentions that four months out of the year are holy. Are these four specific months, or do they change because of the lunar calendar system? Why are these four months holy? Did God command Muslims to only use the lunar calendar system to measure time?

May peace be with you,
Winston

Email #63 – From: Ahmed Rashed
Sent: Wednesday, August 10, 2011 12:39 p.m.

In the Name of God, the Lord of Mercy, the Most Merciful:
Hello Winston,

Regarding 9:23, remember the context of the revelation (see last email). These verses came down to command Muslims to sever ties with any family member that raised arms and fought to kill Muslims. Those who did not attack or join the pagan tribes in attacking Medina and the Muslim community are admonished to treat those family members with honor in this worldly life (see beginning of chapters 29 and 60). Those who treat you as enemies should be treated as enemies and fought until their belligerence is subdued, even if family. However, those who treat you as friends, allowing you to live in peace and practice your faith, should be treated as friends. Notice the exception clause in 9:6. The motivation for these verses is that the Arabs before Islam made war and peace based on family, clan, and tribal ties. Islam came to abolish this tribalism and enforce that these major decisions of war and peace should be based on COMMUNITY (even if non-Muslims are in that community). However, old habits die hard, and many new Muslims were still thinking in the old tribal mentality. That is why these verses seem so forceful.

Regarding 9:36, the specific four months that are considered holy are Muharram, Rajab, Dhul-Qa'dah, and Dhul-Hijjah. These are months 1, 7, 11, and 12 in the Arab/Islamic lunar calendar. Dhul-Qa'dah and Dhul-Hijjah and Muharram are considered sacred because they are the months that occur before, during, and after the Great Pilgrimage (hajj). The Arabs inherited this great ritual from Abraham and his son Ishmael. However, by the time of Muhammad, this ritual had been contaminated with pagan, superstitious, and idolatrous practices. The Prophet Muhammad purified the ritual to its original pristine monotheism.

Rajab was always considered holy by the Arabs, but no one knows why. However, it is significant that it was during this month that the Prophet Muhammad experienced his miraculous Night Journey to Jerusalem, followed by his Ascension to Heaven. And God knows best.

May peace be with you,
Ahmed

The Verse of the Sword

With Dialogue Comes Understanding

THE HOLY MONTHS AND CHARITY

The Holy Months and Charity

Email #64 – From: Winston
Sent: Friday, August 19, 2011 7:57 p.m.

Hello Ahmed,

You may have noticed my emails have been coming less frequently. The reason is not because I am losing interest in Islam or I am running out of questions. I have simply been very busy. I have three inquiries regarding your previous email response:

In your previous correspondence, you mention the specific four holy months that God referred to in ayah 9:36. (1) However, why is Ramadan not considered one of the four holy months? Is not Ramadan the most holy month of the Islamic calendar? (2) I had heard that the entire Qur'an was revealed in the month of Ramadan, but not to the Prophet (pbuh), since he (pbuh) received it in portions over time. This is apparently the reason or the major reason God commanded Muslims to fast during Ramadan. If this is true, then can you clarify in detail? (3) You did not explain why Islam uses a lunar calendar? Is the reason simply because God referred to it in the Qur'an, and the Arabs, including the Messenger (pbuh), did not know any other system for measuring time?

May peace be with you,
Winston

Email #65 – From: Ahmed Rashed
Sent: Sunday, August 21, 2011 10:46 a.m.

In the Name of God, Most Gracious, Most Merciful:

Hello Winston,

No worries about the "slow" pace of questions. I am here to be a resource for you, God willing. Regarding holy months, here is the commentary of Mufti Taqi Usmani:

"The Holy Qur'an says, "The number of the months according to God is twelve (mentioned) in the Book of God on the day He created heavens and the earth. Among these (twelve months) there are four sanctified."

These four months, according to the authentic traditions, are Dhul-Qa'dah, Dhul-Hijjah, Muharram and Rajab. All the commentators of the Holy Qur'an are unanimous on this point, because the Holy Prophet (peace be upon him), in his sermon on the occasion of his last Hajj, declared: "One year consists of twelve months, of which four are sanctified months, three of them are in sequence; Dhul-Qa'dah, Dhul-Hijjah, Muharram, and the fourth is Rajab."

The specific mention of these four months does not mean that any other month has no sanctity, because the month of Ramadan is admittedly the most sanctified month in the year. But these four months were specifically termed as sanctified months for the simple reason that their sanctity was accepted even by the pagans of Mecca.

In fact, every month, out of the twelve, is originally equal to the other, and there is no inherent sanctity that may be attributed to one of them in comparison to the other months. When God Almighty chooses a particular time for His special blessings, the same acquires sanctity out of His grace.

Thus, the sanctity of these four months was recognized right from the days of Prophet Ibrahim (peace be upon him). Since the Pagans of Mecca attributed themselves to Prophet Ibrahim (peace be upon him), they observed the sanctity of these four months and despite their frequent tribal battles, they held it unlawful to fight in these months.

In the Shariah of our Noble Prophet (peace be upon him), the sanctity of these months was upheld and the Holy Qur'an referred to them as the "sanctified months."

And God knows best.

As for your second question, the month of Ramadan is when the entire Qur'an was revealed from the Preserved Tablet in the highest Heaven with God to the lowest Heaven with the Archangel Gabriel. Thereafter, the Qur'an was revealed in passages of varying lengths from the Archangel Gabriel to the Prophet Muhammad as necessary for the next twenty-three years. So the first revelation from the highest Heaven to the lowest Heaven happened during Ramadan. Also, the first revelation from the lowest Heaven to the Prophet Muhammad on Earth also happened during Ramadan.

As for your third question, before Islam, the Arabs used a lunisolar calendar containing an intercalary month added from time to time to keep the pilgrimage within the season of the year when merchandise was most abundant for Bedouin buyers. Intercalation is the insertion of a leap day, week, or month into some calendar years to make the calendar follow the seasons. This practice of intercalation was explicitly prohibited by the Qur'anic verse you mention, as well as many attending Sayings of the Prophet on the subject. The wisdom behind it is that by following a purely lunar calendar, the months of Ramadan and Hajj are free to rotate among the seasons. This is one of the distinctive differences between the purely lunar Islamic calendar and the lunisolar Jewish calendar. The "recalculation" that the Arabs used to do and that Jews continue to do means that holidays fall in the same season, even though the exact date drifts from year to year.

This is important so that over the course of a human lifetime a Muslim will experience these holidays in all seasons. If Ramadan was always in a certain season, there would be an "advantageous" place to live on the Earth whereby the day of fasting is always short or cool. Likewise, there would be a "disadvantageous" place to live on the Earth whereby the day of fasting is always long or hot. The lunar calendar resynchronizes with the seasons every thirty-three years. Enforcing strict lunar calendar means that there is no preferred location on the globe. This is more appropriate for a world religion that is to be applicable to every people and every age.

May peace be with you,
Ahmed

Email #66 – From: Winston
Sent: Tuesday, August 23, 2011 5:13 p.m.

Hello Ahmed,

Thank you for responding to my previous questions. Could you please help me to understand the following ayahs from the Qur'an:

(1) Regarding ayah 9:60, God listed the type of people who may be given charity. God appears to state that a Muslim may donate in order gain the favor or influence of a person or group. The English translation of this ayah uses the phase "those whom you wish to win over"; why is gaining influence over people considered charity? The entire English translation is the following:

Charities are meant for the indigent and needy, and those who collect and distribute them, and those whom you wish to win over, and for redeeming slave (and captives) and those who are burdened with debt, and in the cause of God, and the wayfarers: So does God ordain. God is all-knowing and all-wise. (9:60)

(2) Regarding ayah 9:126, does God put every unbeliever on trial every year, or a specific group of them? What is the context of this ayah?

May peace be with you,
Winston

Email #67 – From: Ahmed Rashed
Sent: Tuesday, August 30, 2011 12:27 p.m.

In the Name of God, Most Gracious, Most Merciful:
Hello Winston,

Ayah 9:60 lists *"al mu'alafa qulubihim"* as one of the legitimate recipients of the obligatory zakat poor due. Literally, this phrase means "those whose hearts are turning," and it refers to those whose hearts are leaning toward Islam but who are afraid of the negative consequences of becoming Muslim. When this verse was revealed, there were many pagan Arabs who found the message of Islam appealing, but they were afraid of announcing their acceptance of it for fear of either social rejection from their clan or family or economic boycott from their pagan associates.

For example, it was common for people to be thrown out of their houses after their clan found out they accepted Islam. In a tribal society, this was the kiss of death, for if the tribe will not support you, you have nowhere else to turn. Also, many pagans refused to buy from or do business with a Muslim, so again, a person who was once financially set would find himself destitute from social or economic boycott. This verse came down to say that it is okay to help these new Muslims or "would-be" new Muslims with the mandatory zakat funds to alleviate their financial difficulties.

In this day and age, the fear of economic boycott is practically negligent, but there are still people whose hearts are turned to Islam, but social pressure or consequences hold them back. Modern scholars say that new Muslims (especially women) have a right to zakat funds to help them announce their faith and not have to fear living in the streets.

Regarding 9:126, this verse is actually referring to the hypocrites, not the disbelievers. If you see the verse before, you see it mentions "those in whose hearts is a disease," which is one of the epithets for those who proclaim Islam with their tongues but hide enmity or disbelief in their hearts. The context of the ayah is that the expedition to Tabuk (when this passage was revealed) was one of the last major expeditions the Prophet led. Before that, there were many important engagements where all the community was expected to sally forth to defend their homes. The hypocrites made excuses each and every time. So this verse is a reference to how once or twice each year previously, the call to defend the land was made, but they found some excuse and said they feared that the Muslims would lose or be defeated. So God tested their sincerity and commitment once or twice every year, but they failed that test each time.

May peace be with you,
Ahmed

Pharaoh, Jonah, Jacob, and Joseph

Email #68 – From: Winston
Sent: Saturday, September 3, 2011 10:09 a.m.

Hello Ahmed,

Thank you for responding to my previous questions. Could you please help me to understand the following ayahs from the Qur'an:

(1) Regarding ayah 10:92, God appears to state that the Pharaoh of Egypt during the time of the Prophet Musa (peace be upon him) lived instead of drowning in the Red Sea. What is the meaning of this ayah in classical Arabic? The English translation is the following:

We shall preserve your body today that you may be a lesson for those who come after you; as many a man is heedless of Our signs. (10:92)

(2) Regarding ayah 10:98, did God or His Messenger (peace be upon him) ever reveal from what land the Prophet Yunus (pbuh) originated? To what location did God sent the Prophet Yunus (pbuh) after He saved him (pbuh) from the belly of the fish? Were these two different locations or the same?

May peace be with you,
Winston

Email #69 – From: Ahmed Rashed
Sent: Monday, September 12, 2011 10:18 a.m.

In the Name of God, Most Gracious, Most Merciful:

Hello Winston,

(1) The passage in question reads: **So We brought the Children of Israel across the sea. Pharaoh and his troops pursued them arrogantly and aggressively. When he was about to drown, he exclaimed, 'I believe that there is no god except Him in whom the Children of Israel believe, and I am of those who surrender themselves to Him!'**

'Only now? When you had always been a rebel, and a wrongdoer! So We shall save your body this day, so that you

may serve as a sign for those who come after you: for many people are indeed heedless of Our signs.' (10:90-92)

The Qur'an predicted that the body of the Pharaoh will be preserved for future generations. So he did in fact die, but his body was still preserved.

This was proved correct when the mummy of Merneptah (the Pharaoh of the Exodus) was discovered well preserved in 1898, and it can be seen on display in the Royal Mummies Room of the Egyptian Museum, Cairo.

Even though this event occurred over 3,000 years ago (more than 1,600 years before Muhammad) according to both archaeological and Biblical data, the author of the Qur'an predicted that the body of the Pharaoh would be preserved as a sign for future generations, which is nowhere to be found in the Biblical version.

Dr. Maurice Bucaille (who was chosen to examine the mummy) covers the above prophecy in detail in his book, *The Bible, the Qur'an, and Science*. Dr. Bucaille goes into much detail about this very issue and places much emphasis on the Qur'anic claim that the body of Pharaoh was recovered and not left in the sea. This was a key issue with him in his comparison of this statement with the conditions of the mummified bodies of various pharaohs that have been preserved in Egypt. You can read his book if you wish to read the full details.

(2) According to historical narrations about Muhammad's life, after ten years of receiving revelations, Muhammad went to the city of Ta'if to see if its leaders would allow him to preach his message from there rather than Mecca, but he was cast from the city by the people. He took shelter in the garden of Utbah and Shaybah, two members of the Quraysh tribe. They sent their servant, Addas, to serve him grapes for sustenance. Muhammad asked Addas where he was from, and the servant replied Nineveh. *"The town of Jonah the just, son of Amittai!"* Muhammad exclaimed. Addas was shocked because he knew that the pagan Arabs had no knowledge of the Prophet Jonah. He then asked how Muhammad knew of this man. *"We are brothers,"*

Muhammad replied. *"Jonah was a Prophet of God and I, too, am a Prophet of God."* Addas immediately accepted Islam and kissed the hands and feet of Muhammad. (Summarized from *The Life of Muhammad* by Ibn Hisham Volume 1, p. 419-421)

May peace be with you,
Ahmed

Email #70 – From: Winston
Sent: Monday, September 26, 2011 11:46 a.m.

Hello Ahmed,

Thank you for responding to my previous questions. Could you please help me to understand the following ayahs from the Qur'an:

Regarding ayah 12:8, what is the family tree of Ya'qub (peace be upon him)? What are the names of Ya'qub (pbuh) wives and all his (pbuh) sons? Can you tell me the name in both English and Arabic?

Regarding ayah 12:19, how old was Yusuf (pbuh) at this moment?

May peace be with you,
Winston

Email #71 – From: Ahmed Rashed
Sent: Thursday, September 29, 2011 10:27 a.m.

In the Name of God, Most Gracious, Most Merciful:

Hello Winston,

Ya'qub is Jacob, and Yusuf is Joseph. The Qur'an and the Sayings of Muhammad are silent on these details. So many Islamic Scholars use the narrations from the Children of Israel (the Jewish Old Testament) to fill in those details. Obviously, any narration that contradicts the Qur'an or the Sayings is also rejected. However, family tree details are usually preserved. Here they from ibn Kathir's book, **Stories of the Prophets**:

Jacob's Wives - *from the People of the Book*

The People of the Book also said that when Jacob came to his maternal uncle in the land of Haran, his uncle had two daughters. The elder one was called Leah (Lia) and the younger one was Rachel (Rahil). ... It was acceptable in their time, as described in the Torah, for a man to marry two sisters. Laban gave a female slave to each daughter. Leah's slave was called Zilpah and Rachel's slave was called Bilha.

Jacob's Children - *from the People of the Book*

Jacob's sons were twelve men. From Leah there were Rueben (Robil), Simon (Shamun), Levi (Lawi), Judah (Yahudh), Issachar (Isakher), and Zebulun (Zablun). From Rachel there were Joseph (Yusuf) (pbuh) and Benjamin. From Rachel's slave there were Dan and Naphtali (Neftali), and from Leah's slave there were Gad and Asher.

As for your second question, again, the Qur'an and Sayings are silent on these details. He was young enough to be called a "boy" when his brothers threw him into the well, because 12:5 has Jacob using the word *"bunaya,"* which is the diminutive form of the word "my son," so we understand this to mean "my little son." After he grew up in the Egyptian household, Joseph was old enough to be considered a "handsome young man" when his master's wife tried to seduce him, because 12:22 says he "attained full strength" or "attained full manhood."

May peace be with you,
Ahmed

With Dialogue Comes Understanding

THE CANONICAL
TEXTS OF ISLAM

Email #72 – From: Winston
Sent: Friday, September 30, 2011 6:54 p.m.

Hello Ahmed,

Thank you for responding to my previous questions. I have questions regarding your previous correspondences.

You had defined in your June 23 email the purpose of the Qur'an: "The Qur'an is unique in that it only reveals details that are relevant to its message. That is, details about culture or history are only included when they further the goals of making mankind aware of the Rights of God, the Rights of Man, and the consequences of fulfilling or neglecting those rights."

(1) Can I assume that the purpose of authentic Hadith, as well as all words and actions of the Prophet Muhammad (peace be upon him), is the same as the Qur'an?

(2) If my first assumption is correct, then can I make a second assumption, which is that any information that is not in the Qur'an or authentic Hadith is irrelevant? I am defining information as knowledge revealed by God. I make this conclusion based on the fact that Muslims believe Islam is comprehensive, and therefore every aspect of an individual's life is addressed by the religion. Furthermore, Muslims also believe that original messages send by previous prophets (peace be upon them) had been corrupted.

(3) If my two conclusions are correct, then can I make a third, which is that a Muslim should not seek information outside of the Qur'an or authentic Hadith because by definition anything that is comprehensive contains everything that is necessary? The act of consciously seeking information not in Islam is, by definition, demonstrating that Islam is not comprehensive. You had mentioned in the last email that "So many Islamic Scholars use the narrations from the Children of Israel (the Jewish Old Testament) to fill in those details. Obviously, any narration that contradicts the Qur'an or the Sayings is also rejected." If my third assumption is correct, then why do these scholars seek such knowledge?

(4) Regarding your last correspondence, why do many Islamic scholars believe the narrations of the Torah to be true? Since the Qur'an does not give a lot of detail of culture and history of the prophets (peace be upon them), it is possible to falsify a narration about such details and not be able to find a contradiction with the holy Islamic scripture?

May peace be with you,
Winston

Email #73 – From: Ahmed Rashed
Sent: Thursday, October 6, 2011 11:16 a.m.

In the Name of God, Most Gracious, Most Merciful:

Hello Winston,

(1) No. The purpose of the Qur'an is universal and eternal divine guidelines and principles. The purpose of the Sunnah of the Prophet is elucidation, explanation, and example of those guidelines and principles in practice. For example, you have a textbook and a professor. The textbook is the meat of the studied material, but the professor's lectures and notes demonstrate the practical application of the text as well as insights and details that are not found in the text.

(2) Yes and no. If you mean religious knowledge and how to get closer to God's mercy and distanced from God's wrath, then yes. The Qur'an and Sunnah are necessary and sufficient for all that any human being may need. If you mean worldly knowledge, such as science, history, and so on, then no. The Qur'an and Sunnah advise Muslims to look at the world and discover its wonders and to look at history and glean its lessons, but they are not meant to be science books or history books. They are meant to guide man to God's felicity and mercy, so any reference to the natural world or historical events are only to further that goal. Muslims excelled in science, and they were one of the first groups to take a critical study of history, so there is no inconsistency between gaining religious knowledge and gaining worldly knowledge.

(3) No, since your previous two assumptions are not correct. Scholars report what the People of the Book said not to educate Muslims as to what really happened but rather to faithfully report what previous peoples have said. This is a subtle but important difference, and it is this that made Muslims pioneer historians. They did not just report what they thought was true, which is what most historians did up to that time. Instead, they reported all that was said about any given event and the details and proofs and eyewitness accounts for those events and let the reader draw their own conclusions.

(4) I did not say they believe those narrations to be true. They simply reported what the Jews said about their own prophets. The Prophet Muhammad said, *"Do not accept the texts of the People of the Book, but do not deny them either."* The understanding is that the Jewish and Christian scriptures are a mix of truth and falsehood, so we can look at them so long as we filter out anything that contradicts the Qur'an, the Sunnah, or known facts about nature or historical events. For those historical details that are not confirmed or denied by the Qur'an, the scholars simply begin with "the Jews say..." and "the Christians say..." and end with "and God knows best." The point is that Muslim scholars faithfully report what other nations say about various historical details, but since they are not confirmed or denied by Qur'an, believing them or disbelieving them does not bring one any closer to heaven or hell. So in one sense, they are bits of trivia. However, out of respect, we say "God knows best" until we have additional information (archaeology or documents, for example) that allow us to make a decisive evaluation of whether any given statement is true or not.

May peace be with you,
Ahmed

Email #74 – From: Winston
Sent: Friday, October 7, 2011 6:55 p.m.

Hello Ahmed,

Thank you for responding to my previous questions. I have questions regarding your previous correspondence.

I wish to clarify one of the questions in my last email. You had given me a very concise and simple explanation of the message of the Qur'an, which is "the Rights of God, the Rights of Man, and the consequences of fulfilling or neglecting those rights." According to Islam, if a person understood this message, he or she will have obtained "universal and eternal divine guidelines and principles." The Prophet Muhammad (peace be upon him) explained how to apply these guidelines and principles in daily life. These guidelines and principles define a comprehensive ethical system. Since anything that is comprehensive lacks nothing, then by definition all the moral guidance an individual will ever need is within the Islamic ethical system. Since the sources of Islam are the Qur'an and authentic Hadith, is it forbidden for Muslims to seek moral guidance anywhere outside these two sources?

May peace be with you,
Winston

Email #75 – From: Ahmed Rashed
Sent: Thursday, October 13, 2011 8:57 a.m.

In the Name of God, Most Gracious, Most Merciful:
Hello Winston,

You have provided a very good summary of the Islamic moral worldview. The Qur'an and the Sunnah are in fact seen as comprehensive and complete. This is explicitly stated in the Qur'an 5:3 and by the Prophet at his Farewell Sermon. So explicitly, looking elsewhere for moral guidance is not necessary. To say it is forbidden is not quite accurate.

Many Muslim scholars and philosophers translated the ancient Greek and Indian texts on philosophy and medicine and economics and political theory. When translating them, they took any ideas therein and measured them against the standard of the Qur'an and Sunnah. Often, they would find ideas and beliefs that were contrary to the spirit and the letter of those two authoritative sources, so they would refute them. However, sometimes they would find a new idea or moral that was not explicitly in the Qur'an or Sunnah but could be DERIVED FROM the Qur'an and Sunnah with appropriate exegesis.

In other words, Muslims do not claim that they have a monopoly on truth. Rather, we say we have been given something of the truth, and if someone else states a truth in a different way that does not contradict the fundamental core principles found in the Qur'an and Sunnah, there is no harm for Muslims to adopt it.

May peace be with you,
Ahmed

Email #76 – From: Ahmed Rashed
Sent: Thursday, November 3, 2011 9:07 a.m.

In the Name of God, Most Gracious, Most Merciful:

Hello Winston,

I have not heard from you in several weeks, my friend, so I'm just checking in to see if everything's okay.

May peace be with you,
Ahmed

Email #77 – From: Winston
Sent: Monday, November 7, 2011 6:55 p.m.

Hello Ahmed,

Thank you for reaching out to me. I actually finished reading the Qur'an a month ago. As mentioned back in June, I was reading ahead of our discussions, writing down questions as I went. That way I would have time to try to find explanations on my own before contacting you. I found the Qur'an much easier to understand after Surah 13; the language is more straightforward, and the commentaries I found on other websites were sufficient to explain what I had read.

Thank you, Ahmed, for responding to all my questions. I need to spend some time in prayer and doing some more research. If it is God's will, He will let me know.

May peace be with you,
Winston

Email #78 – From: Ahmed Rashed
Sent: Tuesday, November 8, 2011 11:24 a.m.

In the Name of God, Most Gracious, Most Merciful:

Hello Winston,

Of course, I understand. Most Qur'an students notice that the first third of the Qur'an is where most of the social, legal, and political rulings reside, so it is this section of the Qur'an that generates the most questions and discussions. The remaining two thirds deal more with the stories of the previous prophets and general spiritual and moral admonitions, so it is less dependent on historical context.

If you feel the need to share ideas or reflections with someone, know that I am here for you.

May the peace and the blessings of God be with you,
Ahmed

With Dialogue Comes Understanding

A Message From the Author

"You will never understand a man until you walk a mile in his shoes."

I thank you for walking another mile with me on my journey of interfaith conversations. This conversation with Winston was the longest-running exchange I have ever had in my work as an outreach volunteer. One of the recurring themes in this conversation is the theme of scriptural context. It is very common nowadays to criticize Islam by lifting one or more verses from the book and judging it with a post-modern bias.

My Christian and Jewish colleagues remind me that this occurs with their scriptures as well. Unfortunately, there is a common assumption that scripture should conform to the modern world and be informed from the same set of assumptions. However, even if a scripture claims to be universal, there is no doubt among theologians of all faith traditions that each book has to be examined from its particular historical context. The Qur'an especially must be read and understood from in this way because it was revealed over a period of twenty-three years.

The piece-by-piece revelation of the Qur'an is suited for the kind of interactive dialogue that God intended to happen with his Prophet *and the Prophet's followers*. Often, revelation would come down in response to some problem or issue or question, so the revelations instruct the Muslims who first followed the Prophet and all subsequent generations. This is why sometimes the Qur'an addresses mundane problems like indiscreet children (Surah 24), rude dinner guests (Surah 33), men and women who gossip (Surah 49), and neglectful husbands (Surah 58). Some mundane problems are universal enough and socially disruptive enough to warrant immortalization in scripture.

Muslim scholars teach us that this is so all future generations will benefit from these admonitions, regardless of time or cultural background. More importantly, our scholars teach us that knowing the Reason for Revelation (the context) is a prerequisite for understanding the message that God is relating in any particular passage. When the context is a belligerent treaty-breaking tribe (as was the case for most of Surah 9 and Surah 8), the verses are understood to be applicable only against future belligerent tribes or nations. Likewise, when the context is general guidelines or principles (as was the case for most of the Qur'an), the verses are understood to be applicable in general, thus forming the normative teachings of Islam. This concept alone addresses most of the misconceptions about the Qur'an being a book of intolerance or Islam being a religion of violence.

* * * * *

If you enjoyed the book, please spread the word about it to your friends and contacts. If you have the time and inclination, it would be **great** if you would leave a review. Word-of-mouth is crucial for any author to succeed, so even if it is just a sentence or two, it would make all the difference and would be *very much* appreciated!

You can find more information and updates at out our website, WhatWouldAMuslimSay.net. Sign up to receive exclusive conversations that didn't make it into the series, free eBooks, my Islam101 slideshows, previews of upcoming books, and other relevant links and resources on Islam.

May peace be with you,
Ahmed Lotfy Rashed

Interfaith Dialogues and Debates
What Would a Muslim Say?
Volume 3

by

Ahmed Lotfy Rashed

Coming April 2018

If you loved THE QUR'AN DISCUSSIONS *and can't wait for more, read on for a preview of the next book in the series.*

The next book contains conversations from 2011 to 2016. In this volume, the correspondents are devout Christians; some are ecumenical and sympathetic, some are evangelical and confrontational, and some are in between. Here are some of the initial email questions to pique your interest!

Email #02 – From: Kerry
Sent: Monday, September 12, 2011 11:28 a.m.

Is there some problem Muslims have with Jews? I kind of understand the Palestine-Israel conflict, but it seems like the tension between the two goes deeper.

Email #02 – From: Roland
Sent: Sunday, October 2, 2011 1:18 p.m.

Dear Ahmed,
What is creation for? Is it just an experiment on God's part? Is it an amusement or a playful diversion? If God is perfect, then why does he need us as, imperfect as we are? Of course, he could correct us, but is he waiting for us to self-correct individually? Is it beyond us, or did He tell us and we missed the point? Stand firm in faith, as it is all any of us can have. We can do good things here, and things can turn out good eventually.
Best Regards,
Roland

Email #02 – From: Mark
Sent: Tuesday, November 1, 2016 6:16 p.m.

Do you think the shroud provides proof of Christ's crucifixion and resurrection?
http://www.4shared.com/web/preview/pdf/qAV-W_Wrce
https://www.youtube.com/watch?v=8YbSaPRuU0M
Shukran,
Mark

Email #02 – From: Nancy
Sent: Thursday, September 29, 2011 7:38 a.m.

Islam is confusing. Right now Iran is going to execute a Christian pastor, all because he refused to recant his Christian beliefs and convert to Islam. Islam is forcing him to convert to Islam. Islam therefore is a vile religion.
http://www.foxnews.com/world/2011/09/28/iranian-pastor-faces-execution-for-refusing-to-recant-christian-faith/
This is why Islam cannot be the religion of peace, as you try to claim. I'm not talking about terrorists; I'm talking about duly elected governments. Even in Pakistan, Egypt, and all these Muslim countries — all they think about is killing people who don't follow their way of thinking. Islam is like the mafia, and I am sorry, but you are telling the West a pack of lies about Islam. I know Muslims who have converted to Christianity and are persecuted mercilessly by your clerics.

Email #02 – From: Neil
Sent: Wednesday, September 16, 2015 3:52 p.m.

Mr. Rashed,
Thank you for the introduction. I do have a few questions. What is meant exactly by "remembrance of God?" I hear that term a lot and am not sure what is meant by that exactly. Why would an omnipotent being have a need or care whether we remember him or not?
Also, Muslims believe that there were thousands of prophets, so does Islam have a means of determining who was a prophet and who is just claiming himself a prophet? Were women ever considered prophets? Exactly which prophets from the Bible does Islam believe and which does Islam reject? Does a prophet self-identify as a prophet?
Finally, why is belief in angels so critical?
Thank you in advance,
Neil

TOUGH QUESTIONS AND HONEST ANSWERS ABOUT THE WORLD'S FASTEST-GROWING AND MOST CONTROVERSIAL FAITH

TOP 15 TOUGH QUESTIONS ON ISLAM

AHMED LOTFY RASHED

Get your FREE copy when you sign up to the author's email list!

GET IT HERE:
www.WhatWouldAMuslimSay.net

MY TEACHER WAS AHMED RASHED. WE SPENT A LOT OF TIME GOING THROUGH THE QUR'AN. AFTER THAT I STARTED TO UNDERSTAND MUSLIMS MUCH BETTER.
—A FORMER ISLAM-101 STUDENT

About the Author

Ahmed Lotfy Rashed was born in Egypt and raised in Maryland. He studied physics at the University of Maryland Baltimore County. While there, he was on the Speakers Bureau for the Muslim Students' Association. He continued his education in Pennsylvania, earning his Masters' degree at Bryn Mawr College.

During his three years of graduate study, he served as Public Relations Officer for the Muslim Students' Association. It was at this time that Ahmed started talking about Islam at various churches, temples, and schools. He became known for his informal and approachable demeanor. His ability to break down complex religious and historical contexts for audiences earned him high reviews. He also taught math and science at the local Islamic School. In addition, he led the Youth Committee of the local mosque in Villanova. Soon after graduating, he married and found employment in Boston as a research engineer.

Since coming to Boston in 2004, he has been an active volunteer at several mosques in the Greater Boston Area. He has been the head instructor for the local Islam101 class since 2006. Also, he has been a volunteer for WhyIslam.org since 2009. He has presented Islam at schools and churches, and he has hosted visits to several major mosques in the area.

Ahmed continues to work and live in the Greater Boston Area with his wife and three children. In his spare time, he likes to read about comparative religions, Islamic law, Islamic history, and military history. He also has a weakness for fantasy and science fiction novels — a problem of which his wife is still trying very hard to cure him.

www.ingramcontent.com/pod-product-compliance
Lightning Source LLC
Chambersburg PA
CBHW050539300426
44113CB00012B/2180